what they are sayir

Heritage Writing

Marie Gass's **Heritage Writing** is key to unlocking treasures from within your own past. Her easy-to-follow instructions propel even the most hesitant of writers to describe ordinary personal anecdotes and discover them to be pure gold.

If you've ever envied someone else's interesting life, this is a sure-fire chance to put your very own into a form that reveals it to be every bit as fascinating!
      Teresa Kao, President, Northwest Association of
          Book Publishers and author, *The Quality of*
          the Light and *ShadowFLOW*

Heritage Writing invites us to create, compose, and preserve our family stories. This book offers its participants practical ways to celebrate the storyteller of all ages within us.
      Edna Kovacs, author, *Writing Across Cultures*

Marie Gass is a gifted writer and a marvelous teacher. Here she helps us learn how to pass on the only inheritance that really matters: a sense of who we are, where we came from, and what we love enough to pass on.
      Teresa Jordan, author, *Riding the White Horse Home*

HERITAGE WRITING

HERITAGE WRITING
SHORT AND SIMPLE WAYS TO HAND DOWN YOUR STORY

by

Marie Thérèse Gass

Sieben Hill					Clackamas, Oregon

Sieben Hill
P.O. Box 243
Clackamas, Oregon 97015-0243

© 1996 by Marie Thérèse Gass

All rights reserved. No part of this book may be reproduced or transmitted in any form or by any means, electronic or mechanical, including photocopying, recording, or information storage/retrieval system, without the written permission of the author, with the exception of brief quotations used in reviews.

Library of Congress Catalog Card Number: 96-60494

ISBN: 0-9651816-4-2
First edition

A similar version of "Growing Z's" was previously printed in The Oregonian.

Permission from HarperCollins to reprint lines from "Keeping a Journal" by William Statford (© 1987) is gratefully acknowledged.

Layout and design by DIMI PRESS
Cover design by M.T. Gass
Cover photo by John J. Mildenberger

AUTHOR'S PREFACE

Anyone can do Heritage Writing. Heritage Writing is simply putting on paper what you remember about your life and the lives of those who have touched you.

Heritage Writing is not genealogy, making family trees or doing research for lost generations. It is not writing polished short stories with beginnings, middles, and ends. It is not necessary to be an English major or have perfect spelling in order to do Heritage Writing.

Heritage Writing is relaxing, enjoyable, exciting. Heritage Writing is fun. If you cannot read or write and someone is reading this book to you, if you are disabled and cannot write or type, you can preserve your memories on tape and ask someone else to type them for you— —or not. Though in the past we received most of our information on books, because of audio and video technology that no longer is necessary. You can make copies of tapes for future generations as easily as you can copy paper.

Your own memories are important. It does not matter that you may remember an incident differently from the way your sister or brother remembers it; in Heritage Writing, it is *your* experience that counts.

Why write about the past? For ourselves. For our children and grandchildren. To learn from it. "I ain't important," one teenager told me. Yes, you are. We are all important. And it is never too early to begin recording memories.

CONTENTS

Author's Preface..7
Introduction..11

PREPARING TO WRITE

I. Why preserve your memories?...17

II. Getting in the mood:

    1. What if I hate to write?..21
    2. What if I can't think of anything to write?............23
    3. What if I don't know grammar rules, can't spell, and my handwriting is awful?......................29
    4. What if nobody wants to hear my stories?.........33

III. Conquering the fear of writing:

    5. Believing that I can write....................................35
    6. Stimulating my memory for facts, details, and relevant emotions..39
    7. Dealing with relatives who remember incidents differently...47
    8. Family secrets and other private things.............49
    9. Putting the first words on the page....................51
    10. Completing the memory....................................55

WRITING

IV. What to write:

    11. Lists and Descriptions.......................................59
    12. Brief Autobiographies..67
    13. Letters 71
    14. Journals and Diaries..77

15. Poetry and Rap...83
16. Stories, Issues..85
17. Slices of Life..89
18. The ABC Method..95

V. How to do it:

19. Ideas, Devices...103
20. Using Your Feelings, Emotions......................131
21. Guidelines for Writing...................................137
22. Variations on your POV (point of view)........141

HAVING WRITTEN

VI. Where to go from here:

23. Sharing, Groups, and Critique......................149
24. About Genealogy...157
25. Adding drawings, photos..............................165
26. Copying, printing memory–stories................169
27. Heritage boxes and games............................170
28. Writing with your children...........................173
29. Writing stories to sell....................................177
30. Last words...179

VII. Favorite Related Materials.............................181

INTRODUCTION

In 1982 when I had cancer and was bored during convalescence, I began keeping a journal. As will happen with you, the more I wrote, the more I thought of to write about. A few years later I began to write memories and keep them in an ABC file, and the same thing happened: every time I wrote about a person, an issue, or an incident, it reminded me of several more.

At the time I was working with at–risk older teens so I incorporated several exercises and lessons about Heritage Writing into the classwork. It seemed that everyone I spoke to about Heritage Writing was interested. By 1992 I was teaching Heritage Writing to several very different groups: all ages of adults interested in genealogy; college–educated adults interested in preserving their own stories; Moms groups who wanted short writing methods that could be used while taking care of toddlers; single teen mothers with custody of their children; and teen fathers who are still incarcerated. The value of handing down memories became important to each of them.

People who had heard me speak kept giving my name to others who would stop me at gatherings to ask how to do Heritage Writing. I searched for texts that would eliminate the major problem of would–be memory-story writers: how to overcome the fear of putting words on the page. A book of tactics to overcome writing–adequacy doubts, combined with many ideas, story–starters, methods, a discussion of alternative ways to preserve memories, plus a select bibliography, didn't exist. It was time to put all my class notes together in a book for convenience's sake.

I still enjoy adding to my own collection of stories and am pleased to have written a book of memories to share with my children and future grandchildren.

I wish you excitement and enjoyment in collecting your own stories.

Marie Thérèse Gass

August 10, 1994

*dedicated
to my children*

Teri, Dave, and Tanya

PREPARING TO WRITE

I. WHY PRESERVE YOUR MEMORIES?

There's nothing in my life worth remembering," a teen father told me at a youth detention center. Some adults feel the same way. Those of us who have been around since the 30s know from experience that our great-grandparents', grandparents', parents', and possibly our own early lives were basically the same. In my case, we all had wood or earthen stoves, lived on a farm, raised our own food and made our own clothes and entertainment. The change from that to our grandchildren's lives today in the 90s is mind-blowing. The changes just from one month to the next in technology, products, drugs, and teen street language are enough to surprise me.

If I am still fascinated by my grandmother's stories of her childhood in a village in Hungary, of what they had to wear, what their school was like, their cottage industries, what food they ate—even though many things were the same as when I was a child, think of how interesting your life as a child might be to your children (when they are young or old enough to appreciate it), your life today to future generations.

By writing your memories, you leave your mark on the world. You say: I am this person, I lived this way, I cared about these things—I am important. When you write your stories, others are affected, even if no one sees the stories until after you die. You have some control over what others think about you if you tell your own true and honest story. Then what appears on the surface will not matter. You can be eccentric and reticent and live alone in a haunted house, but when you share your stories, people will know about the beautiful soul inside of you. And that there is no one who does not have some beauty in him or her. This is verified to me every time I teach a class—whether the person has a PhD and is a generous dynamo of energy, or whether he/she is a kid who has just come off drugs for the first time in 5 years and awakened in a mental institution or jail. Believe it. You are important.

You don't have any living relatives or children, and don't intend to have a family, you say? There is no such thing as a rigid concept of family in the 90s. Families are a mother, a father, and 2.5 children; they are singles with or without children; adoptive parents; two persons of the same sex (which has nothing to do with pedophilia); orphaned brothers and sisters; but also families are those who care about us, even if they are not blood relatives. Families are those whom we care about and who care about us. Somewhere, someone cares about you. If (and I am sorry if this is true) not now, someone *will* care when they read your stories. They can't help it.

OTHER REASONS TO WRITE YOUR STORIES

Writing is a form of therapy, of clarification and evaluation of the past. If I write about how my brother seems to me and how hurt I feel that he never calls, writes, or visits me, somewhere in describing his life as I know it, I will understand better what makes him act that way, or maybe why it matters so much to me. This rule always holds firm: The more you write, the more you understand.

Writing is a way of recapturing or deepening excitement for life. You spend time really thinking about a subject, about describing and remembering and reliving your reactions to it, and the consequences usually are that you want to do something about it, or related to it. I cannot write about the ring my grandfather made me out of a piece of polished pipe (though I thought he didn't care about me,) without wanting to make sure that everyone I love knows it; that I not only feel caring, but show it. Writing changes us for the better.

Writing is an inexpensive way to pass waiting times profitably. Keeping a pad of paper in my purse or pocket has resulted in many a story gleaned from a stint in line or time spent in a waiting room somewhere. One day I had a two-hour wait in a hospital corridor for a minor procedure I was concerned about. By recording on paper what each of my senses was receiving, I had great details to add to a fiction hospital story a few years later. And don't imagine you won't ever want to write for profit—many famous writers started by jotting down what they remembered or were concerned about.

Writing (and reading) is a great pastime for wiggly children in formal situations.

It is never too early to start recording memories. How you can do that with children is treated in **Chapter 28: Writing With Your Children.** Also see **Favorite Related Materials.**

Writing itself helps us remember. It is like hypnosis, in that once we place ourselves there, inside the situation we are writing about, we see and hear details we had long forgotten. Which leads to more stories and more details. But don't worry, it's not so addicting that you won't be able to stop when you want to.

Writing makes us feel good—it's as simple as that. Writing our stories gives us immediate positive feedback, verifies that we existed and partook of life, that we are what we always knew in our secret mind that we truly could be.

II. GETTING IN THE MOOD

Chapter 1. What if I hate to write?

In every group there are those who want to save their memories, but say they hate to write.
There are also those who *used* to hate to write but haven't written for so long that they don't know what they think about writing today. "I hate to write" is usually said after some negative (maybe forgotten) experience. The fact is, that we usually like what we *can do* and dislike what we *feel unsuccessful at*. Unfortunately, there are teachers who have told some of us that we aren't talented or intelligent enough to write. There are parents who have reinforced that notion. We also have sent self–defeating messages to ourselves about our writing.

Well, today we are starting over.

Everyone can write. Everybody can write something of value. It may not be the same style or words or level of competence as measured against an arbitrary standard, but we can all write satisfactorily. We have to *believe* that first.

You must be *interested* in writing, or you wouldn't be reading this book. Interest is the first step after Believing You Can Do It.

"It's a waste of time to write," one student told me on the first day. "I've got better things to do." But when he realized how much he could tell his little daughter in a book of memories, he became a major contributor during sharing.

This book will lead you step by step, easily, into the joy of writing.

Chapter 2: What if I can't think of anything to write?

READ. Go to your library or bookstore and get books from the autobiography section. Open them and read here and there. "Hey, that same thing happened to me when I first rode a bike!" you'll say. Or "My experience with cats was different."

MAKE A HIP (HAPHAZARD INDEX PAGE). Every time you think of some topic you could write about, but don't have time at the moment, jot down a couple of words on that page to remind you which experience you are talking about, like: "Babysitting Aunt Lulu's newborn cats." See example.

LOOK AT PHOTOGRAPHS. Who are the people in the picture? When (about) was it taken? Who took it? What color are their clothes (if the photo is black and white)? What was happening that day that they all got together? Do you know any descriptive facts about others in the photo? Include stories about animals.

- the flood of 1996
- the 1949 earthquake
- last memories of Julia
- Yo, Teach! + agent ♡
- M+J+B - boyfriends
- (Michael's wedding)
- Jan - changes
- the bat story
- the trip to the US in 1947
- building in 1970
- the lost years
- separating milk
- Fluffy, RIP
- Jimmy + the cows
- [1st car]
- Lynda's present
- the gas pipe rupture
- Neva
- Ardiss
- Sebastian
- Carol Jean + his
- Uncle Jim's slough
- Grandma M. visit (last)
- Spot + puppies
- storming the baby grand !!!
- Eva's new arm
- building the treehouse
- Haystack years
- when the fountain died
- Bossie + Wascana
- "Becky" + yrs. on Oak St.
- Vanport
- Kin Canada + Sr. Denise
- series of later-planted Xtmas trees

HIP (HAPHAZARD INDEX PAGE)

E.g., "This is a picture of Jill, Lisa, and Karen, who are my sisters. I think it was taken in 1989 when they came back from their vacation in Bermuda. Dad took the photo at the airport. They were all wearing neon pink and yellow and green print clothing and we were really embarrassed because it seemed so loud in Iowa! We were going to a surprise party at the LaDeDa. The boy on the left of Jill is her first boyfriend, Carlos. We all liked Carlos a lot because he was gentle and warm and funny, and we wanted him to be a part of our family. Then Jill fell in love with Robby and now we love him, too. See the corner of the dog carrier? My dad tripped over it after he snapped the shutter, and pulled something in his ankle, so we had to go to the clinic on the way to the party."

LOOK AT A PHOTO OF YOURSELF AT AN EARLY AGE. Cup your hands around the photo (leaving some light to see by) and put your face close to your hands. Ask your little self what his/her day was like when the photograph was taken. Talk to the child about the background scene, the story of the photo, any secrets connected with the photo. Write them down, or at least write a reminder on your HIP.

RECALL YOUR EARLIEST MEMORY. Describe everything about it. I have a photo of me and my younger sister in a wagon in the hayfield. I remember the day that was taken. I was two years old and it was unbearably hot. My mother had just finished making me the pretty dress I wore in the picture—white with tiny yellow flowers and one green leaf here and there. I wanted

I was two years old and it was unbearably hot.

to stay in the house, in the shade, but my father was determined to take this picture. In the first place, the metal wagon was blistering hot, so we picked some large green leaves to sit on. Then my father kept saying, "Look at the sun," since he had been told that pictures turned out better if the subject was in bright light. I kept squinting and complaining during the interminable time it took him to adjust the camera. Finally my sister began to cry, so my father said we could stand in the shade of the barn until he finished getting the camera ready. Then we sat in the wagon and looked away from the sun while he said, "One, two—" At "three" we both squinted into the sun, and that's the photo as it stands.

KEEP READING THIS BOOK. Other chapters and sections tell you more about getting ideas for writing. Don't forget: the more you write, the more you remember.

Chapter 3: What if I don't know grammar rules, can't spell, and my handwriting is awful?

Write it anyway. *What you say is more important than how you say it.* Looking over some letters from my grandparents (for whom English was a second language,) I see differences in grammar and spelling compared to what we teach in the United States today. But even at this moment there are differences in spelling and grammar in the English language alone, depending on which country speaks it: Canada, the US, England, Ireland, Scotland, Wales, Australia, Europe, etc. For example, look in a newly published book and you may find "all right" spelled "alright" the way we are still encouraged *not* to do it, but that is the way most Europeans spell it—certainly most English people, and in a couple of years it may be more acceptable here in the USA.

"What's the use of learning grammar rules then, if they're going to change by the time my kid gets old enough to have me help him with his schoolwork?" one young man asked me. Grammar in formal situations is just one of those things we have to keep up with. Like computer software or clothing fashions. Just as with word-spellings in the dictionary, what is acceptable in grammar depends on how many people in how many parts of the country are using it that way. When enough people (and I mean *a lot !*) misspell a word, that spelling becomes officially acceptable according to language rules, and only then is it allowed in formal writing. Shocking, I know, but that's the truth.

Getting back to grammar and Heritage Writing—in my opinion, even though I used to be one of those English teachers who had to correct *everything*, it is far more important that you **write** than that you wait until you think you can write perfectly. Just put it down. Do it. Without judging yourself.

One of the secrets of creativity is just plunging ahead and giving the project some hard work—without judgement. The title for a research-filled book I am working on was chosen in that way: I wrote down all the words I thought might be good in the title, then rearranged them in various ways. No great title emerged, so I added more words, writing everything I could think of about the subject. Believe it, most of the titles I came up with were definitely not good ones, but I accepted each one as it popped into my head and wrote it down. Most of the time, one title reminded me of another new word or slant I could use for the next one. This went on for a month or so. My 87th title was a winner. Now if I had taken my first title, or the third or twentieth, and picked it apart: That's horrible—it's too pedantic, doesn't appeal to anybody, won't tell anyone what the book is about, etc.—my creative brainpower would have shut down right then and there. "Okay," it would have said, "if you don't like what I do, I'm quitting." But by accepting every title that crossed my mind and writing it down for consideration, I was able to keep the creative juices flowing, and eventually the right one turned up.

What all that has to do with you and Heritage Writing is this: When you write down your first memory, if you pick the first sentence apart and correct the grammar and spelling, going over and over a few dozen words until they are grammar-perfect (but maybe boring by now), your creativity will shut off, or at least slow down considerably. What you need to do is say to yourself: "My memories are as valid as anyone else's. I am a valuable person. I am going to write down everything I can remember about this incident (or person, etc.) and not stop until I am finished. Even then, I am not going to correct any spelling or grammar. I will put the memory aside for an hour or a day, then read it again, adding any details I may have forgotten the first time. Still no grammar or spelling corrections. There is a time for these, but it is definitely NOT while you are writing. Wait until you are certain you have written everything you can about the incident. Then go over the piece for grammar and spelling if you wish.

You may chose to leave the piece unedited (grammar and spelling as you first wrote it.) Anyone who cares about you or what you are saying is not going to mind that. We are not talking about getting published, here. The letters my grandfather wrote contain many "misspelled words," but they are so fascinating that I began to not even notice the differences, so engrossed was I in the content, the rhythm of the words. What you say is more important than how you say it.

If you just don't understand formal grammar rules and that fact bothers you, or if you intend to use your memory writings for some public use, first write them out as it says in the paragraphs above, then ask a friend or friendly English teacher look them over. If you are using a computer, many (but not all!) of the English grammar problems can be corrected by software made for this purpose. **Also check Chapter 29: Writing Stories to Sell.**

As for spelling, use your spelling correcting software, but remember that any valid word is accepted by the system. E.g., if you want to say something is "from Joe", and you say it is "form Joe", the software will not detect the mistake because "form" is also a valid word. Use one of those little spelling dictionaries that has only the words and no definitions; it's the fastest way I know to check spelling. Most bookstores carry several kinds of spelling dictionaries.

Chapter 4: What if nobody wants to hear my stories?

That's hard to believe. Nearly everyone is fascinated by stories. That's why we have re-enactments of crimes and news on television—because people want to see the story of how it happened. That's why if you are speaking to an audience about a potentially boring subject and you use stories to get your point across, you will have their attention. That is why we watch soap operas and movies, and read to our children. Human beings love stories.

It is possible that you cannot *think* of anyone who would listen to or enjoy your stories. Perhaps all your relatives are gone, you have stayed to yourself most of the time, and no one calls you on the phone. In the gentlest way possible, I would say to you that it's time to Get a Life! You may have been comfortable without people, but you may also be comfortable *with* them. Nearly every town has writing groups and classes where you can help each other write and share your stories. Share a few stories with shut-ins or the local crowd at the senior center. Read to the children (about things they would be interested in at their age level) who race through your yard with their dogs. Share part of a story with someone in your past whom you haven't seen in years.

If, after thinking it over, you still intend to remain the one person in a zillion who "vants to be alone", that's okay—write your stories for yourself. Make a collection of memories that you can look over once in a while and smile at or draw a tear. Talk to your young self in those early days and tell him/her you understand how things were, that even if everyone around you judged you wrongly, you (as an adult) will not. Talk to yourself about your mistakes and make some plans to avoid future ones. Congratulate yourself for all the good you have done. Dip into the happiness you have experienced on past occasions. Enjoy your writing.

III. CONQUERING THE FEAR OF WRITING:

Chapter 5: Believing that I can write

Now we come to the actual Fear–Fighting tactics. Here are some possible scenarios:

1. I am afraid to write because my teachers in grade school always said what I wrote was *stupid*. Besides, I got bad grades in English.

See Chapter 3 about the English problem. In the first place, no matter how brilliant a person he/she was, no one ever has a right to tell you (or anyone) that you are stupid. To say what you wrote was stupid is almost as bad. The American Heritage Dictionary says that the informal definition of "stupid" is: worthless, as in "What a stupid person." You are not worthless, nor have you ever been. What you wrote may have been inappropriate for the assignment. It may have been unreadable because of poor handwriting. It may have indicated that you knew nothing about the subject assigned. But your writing was not stupid. Nor will it be now.

As a matter of fact, your writing will be better now, even if you have written nothing but your signature and filled out forms all these years. Why? Because you are older and smarter and more mature. You have a more expansive outlook on life than you had then. Learning is not as hard as when you were little and your brainpower wasn't fully developed yet. You can handle it now.

The bottom line is that if we accept the basic dignity of every human being, we accept that we are valuable in some way. Which makes the recording of our memories valuable. You have an insight to situations that no one else can have. If you do not write down what you remember and how you felt about a situation, that will stay locked up forever and no one will learn from it, be happy or sad because of it, admire you or empathize with what you were going through. Only you can open the gates to these things, and that is by tapping into and writing down your memories.

2. **I can't write because I was born in another country and am *embarrassed* by my English. What if somebody laughs at me or doesn't understand what I mean to say?**

There are computer programs now that can translate your foreign language into English. So write in your first language if you are comfortable doing that. If you wish to try writing in English, get a partner to help you say what you want to so that it is understandable to the average person.

Personally, I enjoy reading stories written by ESL (English as a Second Language) men and women because their writings retain the flavor of their home country and give me a better look at their culture.

If someone you wish to share your writings with says he doesn't understand your words, ask him to help you make them better. Or get a friend or teacher to look over your work. There are ESL classes at nearly every community college, with helpful instructors at no cost to you.

But if somebody laughs at you because of the way you write, then *they*, not you, have a problem. Just let them go. They'll grow up someday, and if not, it has nothing to do with you.

3. Frankly, I don't know *how* to write—maybe I can't.

Tell me a story. Tell me about the car accident you were nearly in or how you got your first job. Listen to yourself speak and write down all the words as they fall out of your mouth, exactly that way. "You mean like 'There was this guy, see, and he told me they were hiring up at JoJo's but I dint believe him none 'cause he come around earlier sayin he had a line on these other jobs and it warn't true!' —like that?" Like that. That's writing and you can do it.

A note about "fuck" and "shit" and like words: If you regularly use these words in your speech, be aware that you probably do it from 2 to 6 times a sentence. That's an average of 4 extra words per sentence that aren't necessary to the story. If you hate writing or have a hard time with it, why burden yourself with the extra work? Just tell the story. It'll also be clearer to someone else if you leave out these unnecessary words.

4. I *don't know why* I am afraid to write.

You would be surprised at the large percentage of people having this problem. If you don't know the *cause* for your fear of writing, the best thing to do is to work directly on reversing the process. Read on and pay special attention to **Chapter 9: Putting the first words on the page**. It was written for you!.

Chapter 6: Stimulating my memory for facts, details, and relevant emotions

1. Examine memorabilia:

RECIPES
Look over your recipes, your mother's or grandmother's recipes (or father's or grandfather's). Remember all the times your relatives came into town unexpectedly and Mom whipped up a bowl of that luscious Something–or–other? Write about it. Why do you like it? Did anyone ever not like it? Does this remind you of other incidents that happened when your relatives came over? Any other incidents about cooking? About getting ready for special occasions? Write reminders on the HIP.

OLD SCHOOL PAPERS
Those old papers and drawings your mom saved– get them out and talk about them. As the words fall out of your mouth, listen: that is what you could put on paper, just that way. Or write reminders on your HIP

and fill in the story later. Writing short pieces is a good thing to do during commercials instead of getting another bag of chips.

TIMELY REMINDERS

Go to the library and look up a *Chronicle* or any other book that tells what happened year by year. (See **Section VI: Favorite Related Materials**.) As you read about the events that occurred during your childhood and see the newspaper reprint photos, you will be reminded of things you haven't thought of for years.

I remember the day World War II ended. I had gone to the little store to get a newspaper, and there was such a racket up the street by the factories—whistles and shouting and people dancing in the street. I looked at the paper and was surprised to see that nearly the entire front page was a headline: **WAR ENDS.** I ran home and asked my father why they used so much of the paper to print so few words when they could have saved space by using smaller letters. I had been used to rationing and saving everything during the war. He told me about "banner headlines" and when they were used. I never forgot that. When I see a picture about World War II, I always see my five-year old body in pigtails and a pinafore standing on the sidewalk carrying the heavy newspaper and trying to see what was going on down the street.

LETTERS

Do you have any old letters from your relatives or from yourself to them? These are a good source of what was going on in your family at the time, especially if the letters have dates on them.

Dear Mama,
we are very
lonesome for
you.

One letter of mine that my mother saved was written on lined stationery with a blue and red picture at the top—a little girl at a desk. (There was hardly anything in full color in those days.) It is a letter that I copied from my father's handprinted one, after I told him what I wanted to say. "Dear Mama," it reads, "We are very lonesome for you. Daddy made us stew. We put up the pink bed yesterday. I like school very much. Please come home." It was written to my mother by my tiny self when one of my sisters was born. In those days in Canada, women spent a week to 10 days in the hospital after giving birth, and we were tired of Dad's cooking.

CHARTS, ORGANIZATIONAL DEVICES

How about organizational things or family customs? Save examples to include in your writing. In later years, you'll be glad you have them. I found a chart written on the back of the June, 1949 page of a calendar where my mother kept track of how many gold stars we children earned for things like making our beds, putting away our toys, and not fighting that day. No description can take the place of the actual item.

HERITAGE CLOTHING

After my mother died, I chose a few items she had worn as a young girl and put them in a heritage box with notes for each one: "**This beaded velvet cloche hat was made by Barbara Rist when she was about 17 (1928.) She designed it herself.**"

"This flowered handkerchief was bought for me by Grandma M when I was five (1944) and we took the trolley to Eaton's department store for the first time.

1. Don't play during work	Have playtime deducted
2. Always say please etc.	Give back article
3. Come when called	Go without candy
4. Never be stubborn	Kneel in corner
5. Always be curtious	Do a favor
6. Never tell lies	Spanking
7. Never ruin anything	Pay from one to 5¢
8. Hang up your clothes	Weed one row
9. Say prayers + straight teeth	Cut lawn for 10 min
10. Put away books or toys	Not play with toy for --
11. Tidy your room	Clean basement
12. Close basement door	Be doorkeeper
13. Always obey	Spanking
14. Table manners	Have half dessert
15. Write one letter a wk.	Lose allowance
16. Never mock anyone	Kneel in corner
17. Never be proud	Straighten one shelf
18. Brush teeth	No comics

I always kept it in the little white purse that I took to church. Marie."

A few varied items are better than boxes of things that no one will ever look at again. It is important that the notes with them be explicit, e.g., NOT: "This is my Dad's first tie," but: "This was Jacob Mayer, Sr.'s first tie, probably bought in 1903 in Brooklyn, NY." Add any personal comments, like: "Grandma (Tessa Mayer) loved this tie. When Grandpa wore it, she called him her 'Fancy Man'."

TALES, SUPERSTITIONS, SAYINGS

Did anyone tell you folk tales, old wives' tales, fairy stories, scary stories, fables, or repeatedly say certain aphorisms, like: "Better 12 children in the pillow than one on the conscience."? Were you told stories of apparitions, religious or otherwise? How did these stories make you feel? Write that down, or a reminder on your HIP. When I was a child, I was told that because of the Fatima message, the world would end in 1952. As that year drew close, I was *so* good! —But frightened. During the entire year of 1952 I was afraid to go anywhere by myself. I worried about whether there would be another big earthquake like the one in 1949 (my first experience with one), whether a humongous tidal wave would drown us (even though we were too far inland for that to happen), whether the Russians would wipe us out with a nuclear bomb blast (we practiced getting under our schooldesks weekly, just in case). January 1, 1953 I was so grateful to be alive. I also never again trusted completely what adults told me.

2. Round robin journals

If you have difficulty remembering the past in detail, and you would like to share your writing experience, start a Round Robin Journal. Write down the name and approximate date of an incident with a one-sentence description to jog the person's memory. Send a sheet of paper and an SASE (self-addressed, stamped envelope) to each of those who were involved at the time (don't do this too often, if you are dealing with very busy people), and ask them to write what they remember about the incident. Choose incidents that are somewhat neutral yet momentous for this, e.g., "the Columbus Day Storm" or "Julie's baptism celebration"—not things that would be a source of dissention, like "Why Dad loved Lulabelle best." In the meantime, without having read anyone else's version, write everything *you* can remember about it.

Chapter 7: Dealing with people who remember incidents differently

The Round Robin Journal method is better than *your* writing about an incident first and passing your writing on, asking each person to add his/her version to it and send it along with all the other writings until the whole package reaches you again. In the first place, the latter leads to writers not tapping into their own memories; when they read someone else's version, details of their own may be forgotten. But even worse, this is guaranteed to lead to heated discussion over whose details were "right", since each person is going to remember the incident from his or her POV (point of view). The fact is that nobody is "right" or "wrong" necessarily—each person's memory of the incident is his or her valid memory of the incident.

Just as light determines what we consider to be color, each person brings to a situation factors that will influence his/her point of view of the action. A pale blue sweatshirt can be nearly white in the blazing sun, lavender or greenish under artificial light, medium blue at twilight, and nearly black at night held up to the moon. Though some persons will agree on major facts of an incident, the feelings and way of thinking they bring to it influence how they see it, remember it, tell it.

Nobody has to lie to make that true: it is normal. Try not to get anxious if your version of an incident conflicts with someone else's. Tell your story openly and honestly, and let it go. Arguing about "who is right" (whatever "right" is!) solves nothing and only makes things worse.

So which details do I write? Use the Round Robin Journal results as guidelines only. They are a means of stimulating your own memory *after* you have written your version. Write what you remember, and let it go at that.

Chapter 8: Family secrets and other private things

A couple of generations back, no one was supposed to tell anything that went on at home, good or bad. To have a teacher ask what I had for dinner on a specific night in 1950 would have sent my father through the roof, yet when my children were studying nutrition in the 70s and 80s, they regularly contributed the good and the bad about their home eating. (They did not, however, tell how they put their vegetables in their socks until they got to the bathroom to flush them.)

Today, most thinking people realize that openness has fewer pitfalls than being secretive. It is a matter of researched fact that writing down unpleasant or shameful thoughts tends to weaken their control over you. T lymphocytes (white blood cells) of writers who told "all" to their journals were found to be more energetic after five months than those T lymphocytes in the blood of "surface" writers.

There are still families and individuals, though, who believe that no one ought to know anything that they consider personal about themselves. If you wish to write about an incident that involves others and they are adamant about wanting to keep the incident from the general public, do so for the moment. Chances are that they may change their minds later. Write freely in your personal memory file. As long as what you have written is not published, it should be no problem. You don't have to such persons every detail if everything is disturbing to them—just respect their privacy.

My parents thought things like being adopted, or having my great-grandfather be of another religion were worthy of being kept secret until their deaths. I disagree.

After my parents died, I made other decisions about former "family secrets". To talk about difficult or dysfunctional things is to say, "Hey, I'm human, they were human, and we all have/had faults." It is to realize that support and networking are valuable and that secrets fester and eat at us until they come out in rage or other unacceptable behaviors.

It is a perfectly good idea to write about *anything and everything*. If you find that what you write about upsets you, talk to a counselor about it. There are crisis and mental health hot lines and sliding scale-fee clinics in every major city. You are important: do not neglect your wellbeing.

Trust your memory. If you see a ghost or just *think* you see a ghost, your reaction will be the same. Your experience, your memory, is based on how *you* perceived, felt and acted upon a specific occasion, not on whether everyone else agrees that the ghost was actually there. If someone objects to your version, gently invite them to write their own.

Be happy that you have such a wonderful brain that plays memories to you.

Chapter 9: Putting the first words on the page

It is time to throw out Fear of Writing, that monster that whispers in our ears that we aren't good enough to write our memories. Now that you have thought through the first part of this book, you are ready to be successful in getting rid of him:

In a place by yourself with no distractions, think of a single memory you wish to record (something short, like who your first hero was and why). Take a blank piece of paper and write down ONE WORD ONLY (it can even be "The").

Now stop! Wait. Count to 17. Did anything bad happen? Did hoards of people descend on you and point their fingers, crying, "That's WRONG! That's AWFUL! That's STUPID!" No, they didn't. *Nothing happened— you wrote a word and nothing bad happened!*

This is exciting!

Now write ONE MORE WORD, or even a WHOLE SENTENCE (if you dare) before you put down your pen. You are not allowed to judge *what* you wrote or *how* you wrote it. (Or your handwriting or other details.)

Do you see anyone else judging your work? Again, nothing happened! So you see the possibilities: you can write whole pages and memories and nothing bad will happen! We're going to talk about sharing in Chapter 23, but for now, rest easy in the knowledge that you can write just fine by yourself, thank you very much. Write as much as you want without judging or sharing it. If you want to read it over when you are finished, remind yourself of the rules: **no judging.**

Here are some warmup ideas for getting those first **sentences** on the page. Later you may want add to, or change what you write using these exercises. (Just because you may be getting convinced that you can write doesn't mean that your first try will turn out the way you want it.)

1. a. Divide a sheet of 8 1/2 x 11" paper into quarters. Skim through the following list of words and choose four, putting one at the top of each section: **almighty, dollar, racism, glockenspiel, troops, strudel, leaky, laughingstock, bereaved, zipper.**

b. Now write what each word reminds you of, what you heard anyone say about it, what you read about it, what you have experienced in connection with it, how you feel about it, etc. Use the word in whichever sense you choose.

Example: **troops:**

Whenever I see that word, I can still hear Auntie Kay saying, "Here come the troops!" when all us kids came in for dinner. I have a beautiful black and white photo of Auntie Kay at her desk in uniform during World War II. I don't know what rank she was, but I remember visiting her office once. Her brother Jim and sister Armela were also in the service. No one in our family since then was ever in a war.

2. Using the same directions, use four words off this list: **South America, forty– nine, tornado, wholesale, penthouse, indecent, rain barrel, haberdashery, raisins.**

3. One last warmup. Are you filling the quarter-page? Write as much as you wish in each area, but aim for volume here. No judging your writing or grammar, remember. List: **brown paper bags, mitten, Limburger cheese, flowerpot, vacancy, cedar, self–defense, serving, pamphlet, bomber, lace, vodka, deathbed, warehouse, bee.**

By now you will find yourself writing faster, not hesitating as much before you begin. Now put things away for an hour or a day. When you come back to your writing, start with at least one warmup until you feel comfortable just getting in there and writing Heritage Memories without warmups.

Congratulate yourself on your progress so far. Taste the experience and emotions you are writing about. Add any details that may come to you now. You do not ever have to be afraid to write again.

Chapter 10: Completing the Memory

Even though you have started writing, keep on reading this book, especially through section **IV** and **V**, to learn about the actual writing process. Be aware and record every single thing you remember about the person, incident, or issue you on which you are focussing. Use all your senses. With your mind's eye, look at everything in the memory–picture and tell about it by writing it down on paper.

It is all right to have forgotten part of the incident. I wrote a piece about our Guernsey cow named Wascana (which means "pile of bones"). She used to kick so badly that I was afraid to milk her; Dad often got kicked, the bucket was staved in, and we lost the milk every day. The end of my story said: "I don't know what happened to her or how long we kept her." That's okay. Write what you do remember, and admit what you have forgotten.

One important thing about finishing each memory recording is to jot down **how old you were then** (or as close as you can come to it), **about what year it was,** and **what year you are doing the writing of this memory.** Each of these facts may bear on the details remembered as well as your point of view in the telling of them

WARNING: When some incident has remained in your memory over the years and you start to write it down, it is important to write all of it at once, every detail—even those you don't think relevant, because **often after we have unburdened ourself once of that incident, the details tend to fade out of our memory.**

I wrote once (as an adult) about a childhood friend who loved to make mud pies in the house. I was visiting her and was astounded that her parents would allow this, since mine certainly wouldn't. I wrote many details about what she wore and what her parents looked like, and the dwelling in which she lived. A couple of years later I came across the same surname in the obituaries and tried to recall that incident, but I could no longer "see" the parents or remember whether she lived in an apartment or house, or what. It is better to write everything at once about a memory than to write half and forget the other half later.

WRITING

IV. WHAT TO WRITE

Chapter 11: Lists and descriptions

Yes, *lists.* Lists have been used for everything from memos for the grocery store to warmup ways of keeping yourself writing between professional assignments. We will be using lists, not as a means to something else, but as a written memory in their own right. Lists are easy ways to begin writing, but that doesn't make them worthless.

Let's start with ourselves: **I am....** Finish the sentence with as many things as come to mind. Don't weed out the "bad" or embarrassing ones. Don't be shy about bragging. Just let it all hang out.

When you are out of ideas for the moment, put that list aside and take a clean piece of paper for the next list, which has two parts: First list the closest/best friends you have had throughout your life. Start way back when you can first remember having friends and continue to today. Maybe you will remember many, many friends. Maybe you see only one person as having ever been your close friend. *That doesn't make you bad or good as a person.* It just tells what happened in your life.

Setting that page aside, take another clean sheet of paper and copy the name of any friend off your list. Answer on paper some or all of these things about your friend (you may add more questions if you wish):

1. How old were you when you first became friends? How did you meet? How long did you know this person before you realized you would be good friends?

2. What qualities in this person do you like the most? Why? Have you tried to be like him/her? In what ways and with what success? How did he/she influence you or make your life different? How did you influence that person?

3. What years in your life were you closest? (Example: 1945–47, when I was 5 to 7 years old.) What secrets did you share? What activities? Did you get into trouble on account of your friend? In defending him/her? For what? What was the best time you ever spent with your friend? Did you argue often? Fight?

4. Do you still see this person and are you still close? If yes, how do you think that is possible after all these years? If not, what caused you to begin to separate? How did you feel about that? How do you feel now when you think about him/her?

Here is another **WARNING:** You could write the rest of your life on the material in this one list alone, but you may want to sample other methods, even other lists, so pace yourself. Do enough of each kind of writing suggestion as you go through this book, to feel comfortable with that means of Heritage Writing. Then move on to the next. When you have finished this entire book, choose the method you liked best or even rotate means of recording your memories. That's one of the joys of Heritage Writing—*you* get to make all the choices!

Suggestions for other lists:
- houses you have lived in
- the spiritual things you believe in
- animals you have loved
- your favorite songs since childhood
- accidents/illnesses you have had
- everything that makes you cry
- everything that gives you joy and peace
- the places you have traveled
- things you have collected from your childhood on
- all your jobs and careers
- your favorite teachers/ unfavorite ones
- friends you remember from grade school
- good things that happened to you
- good things you've heard said about yourself
- living relatives & deceased ones
- your favorite foods since 1 year old
- skills you've learned and from whom you learned
- all the means of transportation you've ever used

....you get the idea.

For each of these lists that you write, choose one person or incident and write more about that. Do not take for granted that something on the list, for instance "dune buggies" (transportation) will be around forever and everyone who reads your Heritage Writing stories will know what it is. Sketch it or describe it. Tell what it sounds like, what it feels like to ride in one (bumpy? smooth?), even how it smells. Tell why you rode in one–– necessity? dare? enjoyment? and why you liked/disliked it.

When I first rode in a rumble seat, I thought it was such a neat idea that it would be around forever. Who would guess that a good description of a ride in a rumble seat would seem like backwards time–travel today?

In describing the cottage industry of silkworm–raising in her Hungarian town, my grandmother thought only to entertain her grandchildren. Though she had no idea that future generations wouldn't know as a matter of fact how this was done, what the cocoons looked like, how they felt, the fragrance of the mulberry leaves or the sound that the silkworms made as they chewed voraciously, how they looked so fragile as they crawled onto the broom straws that were propped against the table for cocoon–making, how nothing else but the table of silkworms was allowed in the room set aside for raising them––she described everything in detail, and it's a good thing. That is the only source I have for that specific home industry. Other countries and other facets of the industry detailed in encyclopedias aren't the same.

You are ready to branch out into little stories. Remember when it was next to impossible to imagine yourself writing *anything?* Wasn't that yesterday? Well, these little list–stories will go just as easily. Trust yourself.

Try to open your mind to suggestions. When you have read the directions, if you still feel you are not ready,

EXAMPLE: ITEMS AT HOME

1. Above my computer is what looks like a bronze replica of Rodin's "The Thinker"--one of my favorite art pieces. I went to a neighbor's garage sale, but didn't see anything that I just had to have. Then the lady's four-year old granddaughter put the plaster "Thinker" on the table. "How much?" I was excited. "Grandma, how much is this?" The child struggled to hold up the heavy piece. "Oh, ten cents--it's pretty badly beat up," the Grandmother said. But I could already see it restored with dark brown paint and bronze wax wiped over it, so I gave the child ten cents for the statue and a fifty-cent tip. I look at the statue several times a day while I work and admire Rodin's talent and sense of beauty. It makes me plan for time to get back into sculpture again, but mostly it just makes me feel good. My children will have to draw straws for it after I die, because they all like it, too.

2. Three cabinet handles in the kitchen have clay bells hanging from them. When my oldest was in the first grade and came home with her present of bells, I hung them from the most prominent cupboard door so that she would see how much I liked them. In a couple of years, there were two more sets from my youngest two. I like the way the clay bells sound against the wood when I open the doors to get out a coffee mug or a teapot. I smile when I look at them--all slightly different, in sets of two, hung by rawhide--because I see my little kids holding up the bells saying, "See what I made you, Mommy?" The bells remind me how precious my children are and how much I love them.

3. There is a cross-stitched ovel hanging in my sewing room that says, "Friends are precious." It was made for me by Nora, who died suddenly, with no warning. The frame and stitching are in blues on a cream ground. I still hurt for lack of closure. When I notice the piece, I am reminded of the unpredictability of life, and the fact that you cannot depend on anyone's being there forever.

then put your writing away for a few hours or a day. When you come back to it, start with things you have been successful at—lists, putting one word at a time on the page, listing memos on your HIP. Then begin here.

This is something familiar—five items in your home. List the items. Choose one to begin with. Tell what it is and what it looks like, sounds like, etc., where it came from or who gave it to you, how long you or someone in your family has had it, how you feel and what you remember when you look at it, if you are attached to it and why, why you keep it and what you plan to do with it in the future, who you would give it to if you put it in your will, and why you would give it to that person.

Do the same for the other items. By now you will have enough practice to move on—a good writing workout for this stage.

Congratulate yourself for all your hard work so far. Read one or two of your home-item stories aloud to yourself or to someone else. No judging it. You can always write as much as you want to without sharing.

Taste the experience and emotions that came up when you wrote about your items. Add any details that may come to you now. Be happy.

A final list—perhaps the most important: **What do you want to be remembered for?** Give this some serious thought. Then imagine you could write as much as you wanted to for your eulogy. Do so. Tell the world who you are now and who you will have been by the time you die. Tell us how you want to be remembered. See sample page about Madeleine (my cat—a safe subject. She didn't actually write it herself.) Write about yourself. Then cut the memory to the size of one page by leaving in only the most important things (important to <u>you</u>), what makes you special.

Madeleine

Who is kind, mysterious, and intelligent, who loves everyone, who keeps her thoughts private, but is open to confidences from others, whose silken beauty and soft touch comfort the sad and exhausted, who makes those around her at peace.

Chapter 12: Brief autobiographies

After a lengthy speech about his autobiography, the author said, "That's enough about my book; let's talk about me." Most of us can ramble on and on about ourselves. Maybe there is no such a thing as a "brief" autobiography. Do you remember in elementary school a certain grade that traditionally had to write autobiographies? The students groaned and procrastinated and complained, but in the end, proudly read their selections that told the rest of the class or student body who they thought they were.

Certain details tell more about us than chronicling our whole life–journey minutely. If I tell you that Cousin Hepzibah bought one new hat every spring, drank lattés before they became so popular, and wore overalls when her women friends cleaned their houses wearing print rayon dresses, you would get the "feel" for what kind of person she was. Short statements can say volumes. For that reason, autobiography classes for adults often use fill-in-the-blank forms both to jog the memory and to tell much in a short space.

These forms are generally combinations of phrases like the following:

I am (disappointed that I wasn't born rich), or **I am** (the only child of a single mother), **I was, I have, I saw, I lost, I found, I have been, I have never, I cried when, I was happiest when, I hated, I once kissed, I suffered, I used to, I regret, I collected,** etc.
—and so on.

These are combined with qualifying words to produce phrases like:
I've had some very excellent___
I__ then drove___ and ___
As a toddler, I ___, but I soon found out that ___
The smell of ___ reminds me of ___ because ___
I am capable of ___ but I will never ___ because ___
—and the like.

These are further interspersed with "ultimates"- **my favorite season, my favorite possessions, the best day of my life, the best mail I ever received, the first time I was in love, my first memory, strongest person I know, the kindest person, the worst thing that ever happened to me,** etc.

About half of these "starters" usually deal with your past; two-thirds of what's left deals with the present, and the rest with your hopes and dreams and goals. Traditionally. You are free to change the percentages as well as the starter sentences. This is only a guideline. You are the master in Heritage Writing.

You can try some of these phrases and make up a form (two pages is enough) for yourself. Then fill it out. In a week or so, fill it out again and the answers may be different. By keeping your autobiography form short, you will tell more about yourself than if you had listed all your schools and degrees and achievements. Put in your autobiography the things you think of recurrently, the things you love, your regrets and your fears. These will tell a lot about who you are as a person.

Here is an example of an autobiography form filled out:

AUTOBIOGRAPHY

I WAS unexpected.
I LEARNED early that my sister came first.
On the farm, I LET baby chicks hang from my skirt by their beaks.
DAILY, I milked a Jersey cow, Bossie, in the far field.
I WAS AFRAID TO go out there during a lightning storm.
WHEN I WAS 10 I spilled hay bales off a flatbed
by jamming the gears on the panel truck as I drove into a drainage ditch.

I MOURNED my murdered kitten, neck broken in the snow, and
I TRIED to revive a fallen bird that turned out to be a bat.

MY BEST FRIEND turned on me for no good reason.
MY FIRST GRADE TEACHER died of cancer.
ONE DAY she was there and then she wasn't. Cancer could do that even then.
THE BEST TEACHER I EVER HAD never answered my letter
when I wrote to tell her she was the best teacher I ever had

I REGRET not visiting the NW Territories while Sebastian lived there.
The world will not be the same without him.

IN COLLEGE I practiced most musical instruments for hours, **but** can really play only two.
I HAVE BEEN friends with anyone; neighbors complained when **I LET** a homeless family park on my driveway for three days till the father found work.
I HAVE volunteered a lot, **WHICH HAS** made me rich **in spite of** the fact that I have little money.

I CRIED WHEN JoEllen died and I had been too timid to visit her.
I WAS HAPPIEST the day my child was born.
MY BEST YEARS have been those since I turned 50.
I WISH FOR six simultaneous lifetimes to experience all I want to in this world.

I HAVE COLLECTED treasures from garage sales
I AM COLLECTING memories for myself and for my children and their children.

Those I have loved, I LOVE unconditionally.
I SURVIVED cancer, though my two best friends died of it.
MY LIFE IS slower now and more enjoyable.
I DESERVE to enjoy it, and
I WILL.

Chapter 13: Letters

In general:

"Dear Grandma and Grandpa," the letter read, "Graduation has been a strange and wonderful time for me. I really appreciate all you have done for me since I was a small boy, not just through gifts, but mainly for remembering occasions important to me and for the advice you have given me as well as the moral standards you have role-modeled. So I would just like to thank you from the bottom of my heart for being two of the best grandparents a guy could have. Love, Your Grandson Shawn."

If you had received this letter, would you have kept it? Many parents and grandparents keep letters from their children and grandchildren to read over and smile about or remember when they were little. Your relatives may have letters from you as a child, and they may be willing to let you have or copy them. These are parts of your Heritage Writing that you didn't even remember you wrote! Keep letter mementos from your childhood and earlier adult years in a special place with your Heritage Memory Writing. They tell you about yourself in ways you may have forgotten.

Letter writing is an excellent way to get into Heritage work. Some men and women feel awkward about putting essays or descriptions on paper, but find it easier to write letters to their friends (whether they actually often do, or not). A good way to combine the two is to write letters to your children, grandchildren, or future children/grandchildren.

"Dear Grandchildren," my grandmother wrote at the beginning of each of 57 letters. Then she went on to tell us about life in the Old Country: "Today I am going to tell you how we made linen from flax." Or: "Did you ever see a stork? My grandfather's chimney was very tall and every year the storks made a nest...." and she'd be off explaining how the children would crawl up and watch the baby storks being fed. "That you may be kind to the little birdies, is the wish of Your Grandma," she'd sign it. Or: "May you always respect hard work, like Your Grandma." The letters are short—one handwritten page, each tell of one topic, and are priceless to me.

You can write letters about your life as a child, about items that may not last the century and therefore will be a novelty later, about issues that were pertinent to a particular decade, about everything your progeny (as they zip to the Moon in space suits for the grocery pills) may find quaint. Most importantly, write about what you care about most— your values, your beliefs, your treasured memories. Preachiness is out: to dictate how someone should think or act would defeat the purpose of the letters. These are just friendly missives telling how it is or was. "Dear Child, I wonder if you will know what a boom–box is when you grow up. We used to carry them around in the 80s because...."

Or make up someone to write to—someone who will be born soon and who will be far removed from life as you knew it as a child. Do them a favor and tell them all about your life. It will also make you feel better.

Private Book–letters

A special category of letters is the Private Book–Letters. I stumbled upon this device one day when my child was not available to speak to, and my heart was heavy. At a sale, I saw a crude lathe–plate of wood which reminded me of the one my child had made in shop class and given to me. I had kept it upon a shelf, but one day when we were cleaning, I asked her if she wanted it back. She told me that the shop teacher (whom I knew) had told her it was the best he'd ever seen, implying that it was certainly valuable enough for me to keep. But I was young and brusque, anxious to be the perfect mother, and it upset me that she had exaggerated about the plate's worth, as it was still an inch or so thick and barely shaped. My child lying––never! I spoke to her about telling the truth, and also, I'm sorry to confess, about the shape of the plate not being ideal. She kept the plate. Ten years later I find myself crying at a yard sale when it dawns on me what that was all about. And my daughter was on a business trip. So I got a blank book, put her name in the front, and poured out my heart to her. I felt better afterwards. And it was easier to talk about later.

I have since written in the book about other issues I've felt we needed to discuss, but the time wasn't right. Or things I forget to bring up when she visits—not superficial stuff, but heart issues. "It worries me, love, when I see you working so hard. I know you're young and you think you're indestructible. Also it's your life and I should stay out of it. Which is why I'm telling you this in the book instead of in person: I love you and want only the best for you. It is hard for me sometimes to accept what you choose to do."

If he/she wishes, your child should be able to read the book at any time. It will certainly be theirs to inherit. If I had five children, I would make one book for each child, keep them by my bed, and write in them sometimes before I go to sleep. This is a set of very special Heritage Letter Writings.

Letter of Encouragement

The last type of Heritage Letter is to yourself. It's a variation on an exercise that teachers have used in the classroom for years. It goes like this: You write a letter to yourself in the future—future month, future year, whatever. In the letter you state what you have accomplished so far, what you feel you have left to do, what helps when things get hard or tedious. Tell why and how you keep going. What makes you sure you will make it? What good qualities about yourself help to get where you're going? What else will help you be successful in life, and how do you define success—money? power? friends? peace? satisfaction with accomplishments? What do you really want out of life and what is your plan to get it?

Write these things to yourself with a large dose of encouragement, of empathy, of cheering–on. Congratulate yourself for what you have done well and assure yourself of even better things in the future.

Then seal the letter in an envelope, address it to yourself, and in the place where a stamp should be, put the date you wish to open the letter. Put it somewhere (between a different page of the calendar) or give it to someone so that you do not think of it every day. Six months later or so, open the letter. You will be surprised, guaranteed. About what? Read the letter.

Chapter 14: Journals and Diaries

"Because of my mother," the speaker began, "I kept a diary." "Because of *my mother*," muttered the man beside me, I *didn't*!" According to the dictionary, "diary" and "journal" are interchangeable, both words being derived from the word "day" or "daily". Some people write daily and some don't. For some, a journal is a record of events, while a diary is an outpouring of the soul. I have never seen a journal with a lock on it, though diaries are often sold with locks.

At first, the very thought of binding myself to write every single day of my whole life seemed too much, so I thought I'd wait for something momentous to happen in my life. The problem with that is that the leadup and half the event are over before you realize they may be important enough to write about, then you've lost all those valuable reactions and emotions you experienced during that time. Hindsight is, in this case, definitely not as good or better than writing during the event.

Even when I began writing during my cancer treatment, I didn't do it every day like clockwork. Some days I wrote three or four times; some days I skipped. It all depended on whether I had something to say. Unless you are recording occasions and events valuable to genealogy, that should be your criteria for writing: Write when you want to say something. Of course, in order to do that, you must have the journal book (or notebook or papers) at hand with a supply of pens (in case one gets "lost" or "borrowed" as they do in our house). Then at the moment you are ready, chances are greater that you *will* write.

The audience you address in your journals may be yourself *now* or *in the future*. It may be a mythical "journal person" who listens, or you can speak directly at any time to someone else: "By the way, Jacques, I don't appreciate being called 'Frere'—just because you like it...." That's a bad example, but it brings up a point: Writing a journal is not creating a comedy monologue. You can do that besides, but generally a journal is more sincere. Get the "cutesy' out of your system by writing it elsewhere. When you sit down to add to your journal, it is with the most honesty and openness and trust you have. You are exposing your most tender side in your journal—with the assurance that that book will not stab you back. You are safe. The reasons for writing so personally are the same as those for putting *anything* down in the first place—to record who we *really are* (which cannot be done if you are only dinking around), and to learn as we write, all sorts of things about ourselves and the situation we are writing about.

Healthiness of body is promoted by journal writing, though the exact scientific reasons for that vary with each new study. When psychologists at Southern Methodist University asked 41 middle-aged professional men to spend 20 minutes a day writing for five days in a row, they had a purpose: each of the men had been recently fired. Half the group was told to focus on the job loss itself and attendant traumas; the other half merely kept track of their daily activities. At the same time, 22 unemployed volunteers simply did no writing at all. (The "volunteer" part came in the debriefing.) Eight months later, more than half the first group had found new jobs; less than a quarter of the second group were now employed, and fewer than that from the last group had any jobs at all—even though the amounts of energy and organization each group had put into phone queries, sending out letters, and interviews were monitored to be the same. The psychologists' conclusion was that writing it all out gave the first group a better attitude, gave them closure for the unpleasantness, enabled them to move on emotionally—which showed in their interviews and tone of letters and phone calls.

As a result of this study, they suggested the following for men or women with current grief or disturbances: *Without judging your writing*, record your feelings in a quiet place for 20 minutes each day for five days. At the end of that time, if things are not better, see a therapist. Chances are, though, there will be some improvement.

Somehow, we learn and grow inside when we write journals. William Stafford, when he was Poet Laureate of Oregon, wrote in "Keeping a Journal":

More important than what was recorded, these evenings deepened my life: they framed every event or thought and placed it with care by the others.

As time went on, that scribbled wall—even if it stayed blank—became where everything recognized itself and passed into meaning.

If you are still skeptical, the only thing to do is to try it for yourself.

Journal entries can be as long or short as you wish. It is not necessary to decide ahead of time what the topic will be—just begin writing and see where it leads. Journal writing will clarify your thought processes and enable you to better communicate in other forms of both speech and writing. Journaling is not only a vent for anger and frustration, sadness and loss, but also for joy and happiness. In your journals, pretend you are talking to yourself on the phone, visiting with your best friend about your life. Let it all flow onto the page without judgement.

In your journal, you can employ any form of writing, beginning with the **diary**. For example: "There's no one else I can tell about...."

You can also use:

letter: "Dear Jon, I wish you hadn't...."
reminiscence: "I remember the first time I saw...."
lists: "My room as a teenager had these items...."
dreams: "The nightmare I have about once a month starts...."
daydreams: "Every so often I wish Jill were here to spend the day...."

opinions: "If I had my druthers, every person who drives without taillights would...."
descriptions: "After Mt. St. Helens erupted the street was like the moon, all grey..."
conversations: "Today Mom said, 'I just have to tell you about....'"
anecdotes: "At the Post Office today this little old lady walked in and...."
sermons: "This is a sermon, I can't help it: Washing your hands is too important to...."
commentaries: "The new TV shows of the season are so great that...."
eulogies: "There was no one in my life like Madeleine. From the moment...."
—plus **songs, poems, little stories,** even **cartoons and sketches.** Journaling is a pretty free form.

What about after you've written? Unless you have hours of free time with no other interests, you won't be reading all your past journals every day. I'm not sure that would be a good idea, anyway. Rereading is important, though. At some point months or years after you write, read again what you have written to gain new insights about yourself, to see how you've grown, to notice the changes in your life.

Reading what I wrote at Christmas last year gives me enthusiasm and ideas for this year's Christmas—or just nostalgia, if I have low energy. But rereading always makes me smile as it gets me in stronger touch with what I was concerned about then. It's like reading a favorite fairy tale book again used to be—except this is true. You get to enjoy and experience the good parts twice, and rejoice that the hurtful things have lessened their hold on you.

If you are still hesitant to begin, first sit down in a quiet place with a blank book, notebook paper, or something that can be collected into a booklet. Get a pen that feels comfortable to you (not a clunky one that digs into your fingers when you write). If there are distractions--cars, sirens, yelling of kids outside (not the ones you should be watching!), tune them out. With your eyes looking straight ahead, try to see the very edges of your peripheral vision. To do this correctly, you need to relax your face, especially your forehead—get those concerned wrinkles out. You will probably have a little smile by now. Begin writing what's in your head. Even if it's like this:

I'm scared to start this thing because I've never put anything like this on paper and I don't know what it feels like to do it right.

Good beginning! *Everything* is "right".

Chapter 15: Poetry and Rap

When I first met the class of young men (all fathers or fathers-to-be) at the youth detention center in Woodburn, Oregon, I asked to know their first names and if they'd done any previous writing. One seemingly shy teen (many of us get shy in the face of a new skill) said he hadn't done any writing. As I was about to move on, he said in a low voice, "'Ceptin' Rap." "Yeah, man, you done Rap—that's writing, ain't it?" several youths said the same time as I said, "Of course that's writing." The first boy raised his head and looked at me. "It is?" He looked so astonished that I wondered how many other people think they have never written anything, when here and there in their lives they have been devoted to something that happens to actually *be* writing.

I'm referring to all types of verse here, from the very literary unrhymed kind to greeting card doggerel and everything in-between. The quality of what you write depends on your purpose, the standards you set up ahead of time. If you send a limerick to a poet's quarterly magazine, it will be rejected because limericks are not what poets' literary quarterlies are about. But if you write a limerick for your friends birthday celebration or for your own enjoyment or for a limerick magazine, that's perfect.

It is surprising to discover how many non–literary persons like writing rhymes, or unrhymed expressions of their feelings (usually aimed at a lover or ex–lover). There are so many types of verse that once someone defines them all, someone else invents a new type and makes the list incomplete. Though it is listed in section **IV: Favorite Related Materials**, I have to mention Edna Kovacs' *Writing Across Cultures* here. It is the most enjoyable, easy to understand, inspiring A to Z collection about types of poetry I've ever read. Once you start it, you will want to try some poems yourself—even if you've never written poetry. If you already write poetry, you might want to give it a read anyway. Inspire yourself in as many ways as you can.

You may enjoy going to the library and browsing through the poetry section to note the various kinds of poetry and to see which styles you'd be interested in writing. Try some if you wish. You don't have to show the results to anyone, if you don't feel like it. Write for your own pleasure and experimentation. Many people who don't usually write anything have found that experimenting with verse gives them a pleasing feedback, different from anything else.

If poetry (of whatever kind) or rap flows right out of you and is easier to write than prose, do your Heritage Writing in poetry or rap. Just don't add too many words for the sake of rhyme or "cuteness". Try to say right out what it is you want to say.

That's all I'm going to say about poetry. Read Edna Kovacs' book.

Chapter 16: Stories, issues

Everyone loves a good story. The length of the story doesn't matter, whether it has a happy or sad or neutral ending doesn't matter—what matters is whether the story *touches* the reader.

Your life is made up of zillions of stories. Tell them. Jot down on your HIP the titles or reminders for a couple of stories, and by the time you have finished telling those, many more stories will have popped into your head (at which moment, you will jot down more reminders on your HIP, lest those stories be reburied for another couple of decades).

Some stories are just long enough to create a picture in your head:

When my grandfather and his brother came to Canada from the Old Country, they were afraid to visit the big city (probably Winnipeg or Regina) by themselves because they thought they might get lost, or worse, separated. To prevent being separated, they buttoned their coats together and walked down the street like conjoined twins.

That's not very lengthy, but it's a story. It tells of a problem and the solution. It gives a picture in the reader's mind, not only visually, but of the fears and ways of thinking of young men in 1902 who had never been off a farm and were now in a whole new country across the ocean. It entertains. It is a story.

Every day we think of these little stories, then we forget them again. I look at the computer keys and think of how incomprehensible I thought computers were when I got my first one. It reminds me of the first day I entered several hours of data which were then lost when someone tripped over the cord, and how I learned to SAVE and to get the cords out of the way. Everything around you reminds you of stories, every item in your house, every conversation with someone; even colors or days of the week or things you wouldn't suspect can trigger a story-memory. Write them down.

Heritage Writing is basically collecting our own stories. What about other people's stories? Think of them as they relate to you. If your grandparents, as did mine, tell you stories of their early lives, those are your heritage to pass down to your children. Your *reaction* to others' stories, to world news today, to anything—that is your story, not only what actually, physically, happened to you.

Has anyone ever accused you (even with their eyes) of never letting up on an issue, of over-talking about it? We all have our favorite gripes, causes, needs. Heritage Writing is the place to write about yours. Tell it like you would if no one could interrupt you for as long as you choose. Say what you like and dislike and why, without worrying about cutting the piece short so that you still have an audience. Write for days, if you want to. Then when you have said everything you want to, put it away for a while—days, a week or two. When you read it again, add all the things you forgot before, and take out all the things you no longer believe about the issue. Do this several times.

Believe me, you will be getting more satisfaction by writing about it than by trying to work it into every conversation. You will have a more organized approach to speaking about it. And people won't wander away while you're speaking as much, because you won't only be talking about one subject. The best part is that what you have to say on the subject will stand, for all posterity, right there in your notebook.

Chapter 17: Slices of Life

At a retreat once, we were each asked to write our spiritual autobiographies. I thought at the time that that was a strange way of looking at life—slicing only the religious and spiritual out of it. But I began with the type of religion I was born into, commenting on the influence on religion by the country I was living in. I mentioned a few "list" facts, such as my age and date of baptism and when I started convent school. As I told about each religious/spiritual memory, little incidents came to mind.

When I was in the first grade, we had been told to keep our hands together in prayer position, and our eyes cast down on the way back from First Holy Communion. But when I got halfway to my pew, my eyes fluttered up and I looked right into the smiling eyes of my Auntie Kay, who winked at me! I didn't know what to make of it. In 1945 no one spoke in church or hardly looked at each other-- certainly not on the way back from Communion!

AGE/YEAR	LOCATION	FAMILY	HEALTH	ACTIVITIES	SOCIAL	EMOTIONAL	PSYCHOLOG.	SPIRITUAL	INTELLECTUAL	PROFESSIONAL

Whole books have been written using the "Slice of Life" method. A recent one, *Love, Loss, and What I Wore* by Ilene Beckerman (listed in section **VI: Favorite Related Materials**) is short, unique, and interesting. Beckerman remembers an outfit she wore, draws a casual sketch of it on the righthand page, then tells a story or several anecdotes and a complete description of the outfit on the lefthand page. Try writing about your own clothes, say, the snowsuit you hated being zipped into as a toddler, or your first strapless gown. Use the WWWWWH and all your senses (see Chapters 19 and 20) and your sense of humor. Write about 10 outfits. It will make a nice little booklet and a great change of pace for your Heritage Memories.

There will always be incidents that you remember as you write any "Slice of Life". Include them with your narrative, lists, dialog, and other ways you write your "slice".

As a means of choosing which "slice" you will write and as a brief warmup, tape two pieces of typing paper together from the back, landscape direction (horizontally longer). Make one dark vertical line about an inch from the left of your paper, then divide this area vertically by a dotted line. Divide the rest of the double-page into ten vertical areas, giving more space to categories you might have more to write about. Suggestions for the category headings are: **location, family, health, activities, social, emotional, psychological, spiritual, and intellectual, professional.** Make seven horizontal lines.

Start with the first inch, which you could call **age/year**. Divide your life into seven logical periods. Each person's divisions will most likely be different. Period one could be from birth to kindergarten. A simple set of groupings after that could be: grade school, high school, my 20s, my 30s, my 40s, my 50s. Or whatever divisions you wish, as long as the last group includes where you are now.

For the Birth–Kindergarten line, write your approximate **age** next to it. I was in kindergarten at age 4, but that was because my birthday fell on the right date and I was going to school in Canada. You may have attended kindergarten (or been the age to do so) at 5, 6, 7, or later, depending on own life story.

In the second slot, **Location**, write the city or state where you lived—several, if you moved during this period. It might be a good thing to attach dates or your age to each move. The third slot tells who was in your **Family** at that time. Were all your brothers and sisters born yet? Were you adopted? Had older siblings moved out yet? Were your parents divorced? Of course, you cannot tell every single detail in these tiny spaces, but jot down notes at least, so that you know where you were.

The **Health** slot should list your childhood diseases; **Activities**, your school and games and entertainment; **Social**, whom you played with, spent time with.

Emotional and **Psychological** are closely related. **Emotional** could be how you *felt*—were you a happy child most of the time? Nervous? The **Psychological** category goes deeper—it describes you as a whole, regardless of feelings. For instance, were you generally shy and withdrawn? Were you outgoing and loquacious?

The **Spiritual** category we've mentioned already. **Intellectual** refers to your schooling, job training, skills and hobbies, insights, etc. And **Professional** category won't be used till the stories of when you are old enough to start a career.

Do not expect to start at the top of the page and systematically fill out every slot. That may work for one or two slots. After that, skip around. "20s? That was when we moved to Milwaukie, Oregon." Jot that under **Location**. "High school? I wasn't sick a single day." Jot that fact under **Health**. And so on.

Or you may wish to begin with other divisions, e.g., **City, School, Friends, Jobs,** etc., instead. The Slices of Life chart is your reference chart. Something to orientate you when you write other things. You can add to it at any time.

You can *use* the completed (or partially completed) chart by choosing one of the categories across the top to write your "Slice of Life" story, staying within that subject. For instance, the **Family** category would start with your birth, telling who all was in the family at the time, their ages, and as much as you wish about them at the time. As members joined or left the family, you would add to your story: "Julia was the first one to leave home. She was offered a job in Alaska that she couldn't turn down. It was there that she met and married her husband, Joe, who is also a teacher. They live in Anchorage with little Naomi, so we don't see them more than once a year. Right after Julia left, our last brother, Karl, was born in Damascus, Oregon at the Thompson Birthing Clinic. It was Mom's first experience with a midwife...." Etc.

Sometimes writing about your life in slices gives you a unique perspective that you cannot get any other way.

FORMAT FOR YOUR COLORED INDEX PAGES:

A	B
C	D
E	F
G	H
IJK	L
M	N
O	PQ
R	S
T	UV
W	XYZ

Chapter 18: The ABC Method

This method is how I keep most of my short Heritage Writing, and how most of the people I teach like to keep theirs. It is a comprehensive plan for the English language because it, like so many other things in the United States, is based on the alphabet.

You will need supplies for this venture: a three-ring binder notebook (your choice of color) at least an inch thick; a prepunched tabbed alphabetical set of divider pages; some looseleaf and/or typing paper, depending on whether you intend to handwrite your stories or type them. (Or handwrite them first and then type them.) Add to this ten sheets of colored paper like the kind they carry at the copy machine store. (If you have bought a thicker binder and intend to write a great deal, you should probably get 26 sheets of colored paper, one for each letter of the alphabet.)

First put the alphabet dividers into the binder. Take your HIP and put it into the back pocket. When that

HIP (page) is filled up, you can use a second page for your HIP, or a third.

Now divide each colored paper (of the ten) into halves, vertically (example on next page.) Placing one letter in the top left hand space of each half page, write A B on the first page, C D on the next, E F on the third, G H on the fourth page, IJK (together) and L on the fifth, M N on the sixth, O PQ on the seventh, R S on the eighth, T UV on the ninth, and W and XYZ (together) on the tenth page. These are your temporary cross- referenced index pages. The alphabetical dividers are to help you find what is listed in your index.

The Index works like this: Suppose I want to write a story about getting my tonsils out. The main subject is Tonsils, so I would write the subject-title under T on the ninth colored paper. I had my tonsils out in Canada with my brother Eddie. It was the first time I'd had ether. So my listing under T would be like this:

Tonsils (Canada, Eddie, ether)

Under C it would be:

(Canada, Eddie, ether) see Tonsils

And under E it would read:

(Eddie, ether, Canada) see Tonsils

(ether, Eddie, Canada) see Tonsils

So that no matter which listing I look for that story under, I can find it—under T for Tonsils. The main point is to keep the secondary listings inside the parentheses. The word "see ___" tips me off that what is listed first (Eddie) is not the main listing.

Now for the best part—the memories.

The stories, etc. you file in this notebook may be bona fide stories, or they may be poems, letters, descriptions of items—anything from the previous methods section that you do not wish to file separately in another way.

For instance, under Slices of Life we mentioned your Spiritual autobiography. You could either file this under S in the ABC file, or you could put all your Slice of Life autobiographies together in another notebook. That is what I would do—leave the short pieces for the ABC file. But it's your choice.

Remember, there is no appointed length for these pieces; they can be a few lines or several pages long. You may write about persons you remember, about pets or other animals, about places you lived or have seen or were impressed by, about things you used in your early life that people don't use now on a regular basis, or about any ordinary thing you wish to write about. Here are some examples:

Wrecking jobs (Dad, work)

There was a time when Dad hand–dismantled houses for a living. That was between the time he found out his Canadian teacher's certificate wasn't usable in Oregon, and when he apprenticed as an electrician. I can remember going with him to a few jobs and hating every minute—hauling out the rotten boards full of nails, trying to pack them all in the rented trailer so that they wouldn't fall out later, the endless trips from the houses (usually up and down many stairs) to the street.

The most memorable wrecking job, though, was the one of the first fish and chips places in town—fish and chips was a new idea in this area at the time. The building itself looked all right to me and I couldn't understand the waste of tearing it down just because they wanted to put a gas station on that corner. Of course, I had never eaten there, but there's something about the smell of hot grease and kids that goes together. They had moved the original business next door temporarily, so we could still smell the fish and chips frying as we worked.

Tearing down this place was easier and harder than usual. Harder because we were on a busy intersection and I felt on stage all the time. Easier because the boards were so rotted from grease that they just fell apart. It was here that I met my first cockroaches. They were in between everything, all through the walls, in the shelves, between the grease–soaked boards we took apart. I kept asking Dad how anyone could get so much grease all over the place, but he didn't know, either. Though the food had been removed some months before, the cockroaches stayed on. I was petrified of those bugs, and it took some hard talking to get me to carry boards after I saw the first swarm of them. I inspected each board over and over before I could make myself touch it.

Every time I pass that intersection, I think about that scene.

Before I had a family, I remembered mostly Dad's impatience at my fear of cockroaches, his poorly controlled anger at my reluctance to carry out any uninspected board. I remembered how embarrassed I felt when people in cars stopped at the light would stare at me, and how public my fear of bugs had become. In later years, struggling to make ends meet, my perspective changed.

Today, I feel sorry for Dad, that he had a choice of either doing those huge jobs all by himself, or with a reluctant helper like me. I wonder why none of the other kids had to help. I used to think it was because they were special, but lately I've begun to think it was because I was a dependable worker (not counting the bugs). Dad must have been worried about making enough for us to live on. (Like many children of that time, I don't remember being poor—doing without and making or growing everything we used seemed natural.) I wonder if there is any way of hurrying up that mature outlook—my children felt the same way about helping in situations they saw as unnecessary, until they became adults with similar responsibilities.

(I was about 9, probably 1948—written in 1988)

Gardens (Canada, stars & stripes, nuns, trees)
In Regina we had an alley on one side of the house, a pathway behind us, the street in front, and the driveway–sandbox–wading pool on the other side, so there wasn't room for a garden. The only things I remember planting were the two miniature fir trees, one on each side of the sidewalk that led from the street to the front porch. I was four years old at that time, and the trees were shorter than I was. The last time I saw them, they looked like virgin timber.

A cloistered order of nuns lived less than a block away, and they let Mom make a garden in their yard. There were a couple of extern sisters who were allowed to speak with the public. I only remember going over there to the garden a few times, right before we left for the United States. The nuns would ask me every time, "Tell us what land you're moving to." And for

the life of me, from one time to the next I could not remember if it was the land of the "stars and stripes" or the "stars and strips." Each time I'd think it over, choose the most logical one, and it was always wrong. Then they'd laugh and I'd be so embarrassed. I tried to visualize the American flag so that I could remember the right words, but who could tell if they were stripes or strips, anyway?
(I was 6 or 7, 1947) (written in 1988)

    Notice that each piece has the date or my age or something to tell when it took place. Also a date on the right side that tells when it was written (well before I became senile, for instance).
    When I read some of these to my mother the year she was dying, she added some factual details. I did not rewrite any of the pieces, but put her comments in the margin, e.g., "the nuns were Sisters of the Precious Blood," or "the last year we grew only peas, lettuce, and onions."
    A last example:

Bessie and Mike (farm, Canada)
    A blue bottle fly lands on my leg and in a flash I am back on my grandparents' farm on the Canadian prairie, staying by myself with Bessie and Mike (my great-uncle). I was 4 or 5 then and Bessie taught me the "Jimmy Crack Corn" song and we examined blue bottle flies together. I wondered if they were made out of glass, or why did they call them "blue bottle"?
    Bessie would give me a penny for each fly I swatted. For short periods of time, I was allowed to lower the yellow-painted window (raising the temperature

of the kitchen considerably in a very few minutes) and corner the flies as they tried to get out. There were no screens. Once when Bessie left the room, I was strongly tempted to take some flies off the long sticky yellow flypapers that dangled from the ceiling. I stood on my tiptoes, just in case I could make it before she came back into the room, but I was too short to reach any flies.

Bessie let me wear her blue gingham ruffled apron and make a tinfoil crown so that I could be the flyswatting fairy dancing about. She sternly warned me to stay away from the open root cellar in the middle of the kitchen floor, and not to trip on the heavy trapdoor with its protruding iron ring, but I managed to fall down it anyway. I remember thinking what a quick ride it was from the kitchen linoleum to the dirt floor at the bottom of the wooden stairs where I stayed in the same position, my head against a quart jar of plums, looking at the cobwebs, until Bessie quit ranting and offered me some sympathy.

Bessie was from England, and I loved to hear her speak. Mike, grandpa's brother, ran the farm while we lived in town. Short and stocky, balding and smiling, Mike was okay looking, but Bessie was so pretty! (According to my child-standards.) She had black eyes and lashes, round rosy cheeks, curly black hair, and always wore bright red lipstick and lots of perfume. I knew I could never speak with her delightful British accent, but I could memorize the way she looked so that I could look like her some day.

One morning I got up early before anyone else. A stranger walked out of Bessie's bedroom. "Where's Bessie?" I asked, frightened. The pasty-faced, straight-haired stranger looked at me oddly, then spoke. She had Bessie's voice, but I wasn't at all sure it was Bessie. "Look, I'll show you," she said as she went to work in front of the small wood-framed mirror that hung to the left of the iron stove. By the time she had her makeup and perfume on and had put her hair up in a red scarf, I believed. She did not, however, appreciate my telling her that she looked like two different persons, the unmadeup one so much older. I thought she'd *want* to know, since obviously, she didn't already, or she'd never go around without makeup again.

    I never saw Bessie or Mike after that summer, though that was a year or so before we moved to the United States.

(about1945)   (written in 1988)

V. HOW TO WRITE

Chapter 19: Ideas and devices

Remember that describing items has been touched on earlier in this book. Well, you can make your memory–description more complete and interesting by using these ordinary devices:

1. **Five Ws and an H.**

Take a butter churn, for instance. You don't see many of those nowadays. We had several, from the tall wooden slosher one to the glass gallon–sized metal topped ones with wooden paddles inside, turned by a crank attached to the lid.

If I were deciding what to include in a selection about butter churns, I would look at: Who, What, When, Where, Why and How. For example:

Who: The little kids got to give the churn a few turns once in a while, but mostly I was the one who had to make butter. Mom was busy and Dad was at work, and as the oldest child, I had the stamina to crank or slosh for the half-hour or hour (depending on my cpm—cranks per minute).

What: We used pure cream from the Jersey cows to make butter. It was the best tasting butter I've ever had!

When: When we lived on the farm at Carver, we made butter about once a week.

Where: In what we'd now call the "family room" or "great room"—the large room off the kitchen where we did everything. It was more fun to crank in that room while I read from a propped-up book than it was to do it in the kitchen with all those other chores staring me in the face.

Why: Because we liked butter, margarine hadn't been invented yet, no one (outside of medical persons) knew anything about cholesterol or saturated fats, and my mother made me do it. Fresh butter was delicious on thick slices of homemade bread.

How: The cream was measured (I don't remember how much) into the container, and then I just started cranking or sloshing. The action of the paddles separated the fatty part out of the cream eventually. First I'd see little specks of yellow, then they'd get bigger, and eventually all the yellow stuck together in a pound of butter. Then I'd open the lid and pour off as much of the thin milky stuff as I could without spilling the butter. The butter was washed in cool water then, and salt worked into it. Then it was pressed into the butter form which had four parts so that the entire pound didn't have to be set on the table every time you used butter. It was stored in the icebox—in later years, the refrigerator.

2. Using your senses.
Most items or occasions have sense–memories. Not every sense will give you an answer every time, though. Let's try the butter churn again:

Sight: Describe the cream turning to butter, the churn, the room.
Hearing: The paddles made a sloshing sound as they worked the cream.
Touch: The metal crank warmed up as I went along, the glass container of cream was cold at first; the smoothly sanded slosher, the tall barrel–like wooden churn as I held it steady between my knees both felt comfortingly of wood.
Smell: There wasn't any unless it was a very hot day and the wooden slosher was being worked outside. But when the churn was opened, the fragrance of whey came out. When the salt was worked in there was another slight smell of butter. With the wooden churns, sometimes the wood had a damp smell to it.
Taste: The anticipated taste of the finished product was the only taste.

If you are writing about an *occasion*, an incident, stand in the middle of the scene and ask your senses, one at a time, what messages they are sending to you. The more senses you involve in the story, the clearer and more memorable your story will be to the reader.

Writing about a *person* can also involve all or most of the senses (even if he/she bathes regularly). Listen to your sensory input memory as you write.

They say that each one of us is three persons: **who we think we are, who others think we are, and who we**

really are. Heritage Writing about *ourselves* and our reactions to others, incidents, and things, will tell who we really are. But how about when we write about *people we know*? Which "person" are we writing about then? The answer depends on how well you know him/her. We know who *we* think they are. With regard to some people, we also know who *they* think they are. ("She's always trying to be...." or "He thinks he's....") A few we know who they *really* are inside. These are likely to be our closest friends.

When you write about someone, keep those three "persons" in mind.

Do not ignore the sixth sense, **intuition**. In writing about persons, places, or incidents, intuitive perceptions should also be recorded, both as they appeared at the time of the story and as they are now during the telling of it. Example:

When I was little, an older male neighbor, Mr. S, used to drop by to visit with my mother while she was ironing in the kitchen, canning, or doing something she wanted done. In the beginning, she would stop work and offer him tea. After a while, she used to grumble about his taking up so much of her time, so she would make him tea, then continue ironing or canning or whatever, even though she felt it was somewhat rude to work while company was there.

At the time, I was small enough so that when Mr. S asked me to sit on his lap, my mother insisted I do so. It was the polite thing to do in those days. No one thought of their neighbor as being a pervert—in fact, I had never heard the word. Mr. S was then probably in his 70s, shuffled along slowly with a gnarled

brown cane. Visiting my mother was his outing. But there was something about the man that made me afraid. I told my mother I didn't want to sit on his lap, but when she asked me why, I couldn't think of an answer. Finally, I said, "Because he always keeps his hand under me and I don't like sitting on his fingers." Even at that, I thought his leaving his hand there was an accident. When he wiggled his fingers next to my panties, I thought he was just trying to get the circulation back into them. Nobody I knew would deliberately molest anyone or even come near to it. In fact, I had never been told what molestation was. Like my siblings and friends, I was under the impression that adults were always right. My mother said it would hurt his feelings if we didn't sit on his lap, so I continued to, but one day I couldn't stand it anymore, and as I went to sit down, when he put his hand on his knee, palm up, I brushed it away, saying playfully, "Not until you move your hand." He moved it that time. I don't remember his visits after that. I didn't know at the time exactly what was amiss—nothing, according to rules I'd been taught. But there was something....
(about 7 years old)   (written in 1994)

That is the sixth sense. Tell about it as it relates to incidents as they happened, then also include any intuitive flashes that occur as you tell the story.

3. Picture this

Sometimes a **picture** will help, even a generic one of something common, like a car. Tell about your childhood memories of cars (and rumble seats?), of the first car you owned or fell in love with, about cars you have known, and don't forget to tell everything about your ideal car that you're going to get when you win the lottery. If you have **watermarks** on your software, you might want to use a sheet where the car is printed as background.

Be aware of the places and persons the car reminds you of—these are new stories that should be memoed on your HIP for future writings.

When we first came from Canada, we stayed with my father's aunt and uncle until we found a house. One day, Dad came home with a black (Model T?) square-topped automobile, which I thought was beautiful! It was so like the cars my grandparents and parents' friends had. Though I rarely rode in cars (we hadn't owned one in Regina), except for the rumble seat ride, the other cars I had ridden in looked just like this. I couldn't understand why some of the kids at school would make fun of it. As far as I could see, our next car was the one to make fun of—an old DeSoto, painted pastel pink! I was by then probably 11 and totally embarrassed to be seen riding in that!

One thing about the black car—when we went on a Sunday drive up the steep, narrow streets of the West Hills, from the time when the car would go slower and slower, all of us leaning forward as we strained to reach the crest of the hill, to the moment when Dad gave up, shifted into reverse, and backed down, I trusted that old car to be able to turn sharply at the foot of the first incline and not send us over the cliff. The memory of everyone either squealing or saying, "Be quiet!" and of holding my breath as we backed slowly down will probably stay in my memory forever.

4. Common Scents.

Line up containers of aromatic things. Use a few kitchen items like vanilla, sage, garlic, a fresh herb, vinegar, yeast. Then add household scents like lavender, pressed powder, epsom salts, liquid liniment, iodine. If you have other things around that might have been in use when you were a child, add them too, i.e., chicken feed, a geranium, a wooden container with rainwater in it, some worn leather or hay. Whatever is available to you. Choose five or six things total.

If the containers do not have lids, put a piece of foil or plastic wrap over them. Keep whatever you have chosen separate from the other. Now take the first scent. Supposing it is the geranium. Yes, you know what it is already, but that doesn't matter. Close your eyes and hold the flower up so that you can smell it. Keep your eyes closed and keep smelling the geranium while you let your thoughts drift wherever they will go. Chances are very good they will tell you some stories from your past.

Geraniums: Every summer, Mom put clay pots, each with a single red geranium, on the windowsills of the enclosed porch. The color was so pretty, especially when the sun shone through the petals and leaves. Lipstick red was the only color I'd ever seen by 1947––not like the "blue" and "pink variegated" ones in my yard now. The scent of geraniums reminds me of when I tried to smell their fragrance for the first time. "That's awful!" I said to my mother. "How can something that looks so good smell so bad? There must be a mistake." She laughed and said that that's just the way things are.

Just that much of a glimpse reminds me of several stories: one about naming the couch on the sunporch, one about learning long division on the blackboard that hung to the left of the front door, and one about my getting upset when my mother hugged several male friends goodbye—even though my father was standing right there.

Now try another scent in the same manner. Jot down a few reminder words on your HIP. When you have gone through as many scents as you wish for the moment, write up at least one Heritage Memory brought up by the aromas. Writing at least one story now will make you eager to write more stories the next time you have a moment.

5. Streets of Former Dreams.
Nearly everyone has one place he/she lived longer than anyplace else, or one place that was their favorite, or that stands out in their memory for any other reason. Describe every single thing you can about it, starting when you enter the street the house (apartment, duplex, etc.) is on. Go in the front door (writing all the way), paying special attention to things that catch your eye, i.e., **the back of the front door was done with a shiny brown varnish, but the outside was painted white to match the porch.**

Look around you as you enter the house. Describe each of the rooms in detail.

By this time, stories are crowding your mind, saying, "Let me tell! Let me tell!" Calmly ask them to wait their turn and jot down a few words on your HIP so that you can write those stories later. Continue your walk through the house, looking at it in your mind's eye the way it looked when you were seven, or ten, or whatever age you were when you lived there. When you have finished with the house and the yard, choose one or two stories off your HIP (short ones would be best, since by this time you may be emotionally exhausted) and write them, using as many senses and other devices as you can. Make a specific date with yourself for sometime *soon* to write another story. On the day you write that one, make another date, and so on, so that you don't end up with fifty HIP pages and no written Heritage Memories.

6. How-to

Choose any item out of your past that you were responsible for running, or working. (I hesitate to call these "machines" because most of them were probably run by elbow grease instead of automatically.) Tell about it first, using the "5Ws and an H" as well as your sense input. Then write how to run it, using a 1. 2. 3. system like a "How-to" manual. For instance, you could use a milk separator.

Working in the milkhouse separating the milk (from cream) while the other kids were most likely doing fun things was not my favorite occupation. I thought that if I had to milk the cows, at least someone else could do the separating. My biggest gripe lay with all the washing and sterilizing of the cones before they could be used and after they were full of milk. Once in a while, I'd drop the stack as I was putting them on the pin for washing, and it would take forever to figure out the order in which they were supposed to be put back onto the machine. Nearly every day I was tempted to skip the soap wash or one of the rinses, but my father had impressed upon me that following the directions was a matter of life and death, even if I had no idea of the actual diseases that could result from poor sanitation. So I did everything as I was taught to do them, like this:

1) Set the milk bucket on the sideboard while you assemble the separator. Make sure all the parts are dry and still wrapped in the clean cloth first.

2) Pick up the smaller of the two bowls (with spouts)....and so on.

Not only is it tricky to write out directions in an orderly manner for simple things, but making them understandable to anyone who doesn't know what you're talking about is even harder. What's the use of this? In writing about things we gripe about, we often come across reasons we *liked* the job—forgotten reasons. (Separating milk seems rather classy and fascinating to me now.) Makes for a more pleasant memory instead of: **Separating milk? Hated it!**

Now I remember that we kept a couple bales of straw in the shed behind the milkhouse, and one day there were six baby mice in a nest on the top bale. I remember whitewashing the milkhouse inside and out, and how nice it looked when I was finished. How the cat, Midnight, loved me when I came out with her bowl of milk.

It is also something interesting to pass onto future generations.

When Grandma wrote about grape harvest, describing what was going on in the vineyard, on the wagons, and in the cellars, it was fascinating to me—not because

I had no idea at all of what happens to grapes before they become wine (I started making wine in 1970), but because this was slightly different, this hauling of wooden vats with a team of four horses, because I could see the children who sang and played on the ride back to the vineyards, because I could read between the lines how much Grandma missed Hungary and being a child—because of lots of reasons.

Your own writings about familiar things (familiar to you, at least) will impart that bit of extra flavor to others' lives when they read about how you lived. Make the effort. I think you'll be gratified, even when you reread your own work for the first time.

7. Writing History.

They say that everybody knows exactly what he or she was doing when they heard that John F. Kennedy had been shot. What were you doing? How did you learn about it? Who told you? What was your immediate reaction? Did you say anything? Then what did you do? How was the rest of your day, week, month? How did you feel about the theories of who shot JFK (then)? What do you think now? Do you still hurt when you think about that incident? Why? How long did it take you to get over it?

When you write about yourself in conjunction with an event in history, you put some sense of closure on the painful things, you relive the pride in yourself that you felt on momentous positive occasions, you put into perspective some of the fears you felt at that time, and you see better from here how things were. Adding your reactions and emotions, thoughts, and actions to the ordinary tale of what historically happened will make that occasion more memorable for whoever reads this afterwards. Your spin on that time gives a deeper, more colorful picture of what went on.

8. Edibles.

A simple, but (usually) funny way to approach memories of food is to state what you hated most to eat and what happened to you when you didn't eat it. Unfortunately, or fortunately, children of today don't have that problem much. But back then we were eating for "the poor children in Europe" or other causes, one of the most secret being that our mothers were anxious lest we not get balanced nutrition and they be blamed for being bad mothers.

Pears (Canada, food)

I've always hated pears, even before I tried to figure out why. Maybe I felt threatened by the large number of jars of pears my mother canned each year. Anyway, between the ages of 3 and 7 I'd often sit alone at the dinner table at least a half hour after everyone had left, staring at the clock and the wall, indenting lines into the white oilcloth with my fingernails, asking my mother countless inane questions—anything to avoid eating the pale slippery halves that looked up at me from the proper little dessert bowl. My sister Lulu, younger and clearly the favorite—I knew it even then, would throw her meat under the table from where it was tsk–tsk'd into the dustpan with the rest of the crumbs. But pears—could I do that with pears? In the first place I worried that they'd plop when they hit the floor. And they were wet. The chances of their sliding across the floor and coming to an abrupt halt against my mother's shoes were great in my mind, though in retrospect, I doubt the floor slanted that much.

"Why don't you like pears?" my mother would ask through pursed lips, dishtowel slung over her shoulder, myself being the last impediment to a cleaned-up kitchen.

"They're gritty," I'd say, shrugging. That wasn't all of it, but I couldn't figure out the rest. The color was okay, the taste not too sweet or pungent. I often felt I had no right to object to such an unassuming fruit, and I'd often ask my off-guard mind what the problem was. Never got a decent answer. Even 30 years later when pears were declared one of my food allergies, it didn't seem reason enough for all that animosity.

"Gritty," I'd said, but it wasn't only the texture. I also disliked strained, chilled pear juice.

One day Mom asked Lulu why she threw her meat under the table. "I wasn't hungry," she said.

"But you ate your dessert," Mom pointed out.

"I wasn't hungry for meat, just for dessert," Lulu said, which I in my year-and-a-half-older wisdom thought totally illogical—until she got away with it.

"I'm not hungry for pears, just for cake," I said slyly then to my mother.

I knew *she knew* I was putting her to the test. But I don't remember having to eat pears after that.
(before 1947) (written in 1988)

Writing about foods you hated can bring up related subjects, such as experiences with growing vegetables, canning, or trying out that special dish that didn't quite work—on company. What are your favorite foods? What is the difference between what your mother had in her refrigerator and what you keep in yours? Have you had a comedy of errors regarding food? For example:

Growing Zs (garden, food, living in the woods)

"You must be the only person in the world who can't grow zucchini," the nursery person said laughing. Then she cleared her throat and made her expression serious again. "So tell me."

"Things didn't look good in the spring," I answered. Or winter, which was really spring because spring is really summer because we didn't have any winter in Oregon this year. The last time I grew anything gardenlike was in 1980—I know that for a fact because I was looking in my decorating notes file yesterday and I found the beautiful handbound volume that used to be my garden journal.

"This journal was started in May, 1980," it said on the first page. The next three pages were torn out, but I remember what they held: notes and graphs and charts of when and what was planted, what was done to the soil, how much rain we had, when the plants were fed and watered, and so on. That was the year when, after seasons of no success with vegetables, I decided to zero in on my two favorites: tomatoes and zucchini.

I dug down and mixed soil and ended up with a large raised bed of natural soil, potting soil, steer manure, sand, vermiculite, and lush topsoil. The bed was

10 feet square and raised 12 inches. I waited until the garden column said "Plant!" before buying excellent-looking tomatoes at a reputable nursery. I not only planted them according to instructions but followed suggestions from successful gardeners. I also sang to the tomato plants. Maybe that was the problem. Anyway, as soon as they looked comfortable, I turned my attention to the zucchini.

Personally, I'd never seen too much zucchini, but people kept warning me about it. So instead of planting an entire package of seeds, I bought three healthy plants at the nursery. These I planted in as much sun as we had in the woodsy clearing and tended them as attentively as the tomatoes. By midsummer, the zucchini plants were waving huge leaves around, and some of the blossoms had baby z's attached.

I was excited. The day before the first picking, I watered them, told them a story, and put out fresh slug bait. The next morning, I was horrified to see only slug bait and a few tall stems left on the plants. And one nibbled-on squash. A lot of fat slugs were darn happy that night.

That's when the tomatoes apparently went into shock. Or maybe it was a virus, as a neighbor suggested. Anyway, overnight, the plants and green tomatoes turned to mush. I buried them in their own bed. And since then, I haven't even tried to plant anything. Until now.

"Don't you have any friends? Everybody can grow zucchini," the nursery lady said.

"The truth is," I replied, "my friends are so considerate that even when they grew wheelbarrows full of the stuff, they'd say, 'Everybody has so much zucchini— the last thing you'd want is one of these.' And they'd bury the load in the compost."

"How many seeds did you plant?' the nursery woman asked.

"Twenty-seven," I answered.

"Twenty-seven?" she guffawed, grabbing a passing co-worker. "This lady planted 27 zucchini plants!" They hooted, finally pulling themselves together to inform me that I should have enough zucchini for a small country.

"I only wish," I said sadly. "But not a single seed has come up, and it's been six weeks."

"Six weeks?" Laughter got the best of them. "What'd you do, plant them upside down?" And they were off into hysterics again. "No, I guess you can't do that," said one of them, wiping away the tears and trying to look businesslike. "Tell me exactly what you did."

So I told them about starting the zucchinis in new seed pots with greenhouse covers in the sunroom, about the soil, food, water, drainage, where and when I bought the seeds. But not about the singing.

"And you don't have a single plant up?" They shook their heads with me.

"What should I do?" I asked.

"Give up," they responded, smiles ready to break open again. Then they changed their minds. "No— wait. Buy some plants. There's no way the seeds will come up now."

Were they ever wrong! Four days later, six little leaves poked out with the seed pods still on their heads. I transplanted them and was astounded to see masses of roots. "So that's what you've been doing," I muttered, then put on a pleasant expression. I sang to them under my breath then, because the neighbors were out in the yard.

To cut a long story short, 13 plants lived after I switched three brands of slug bait and sheltered them in jars. Most of the plants have blossoms. I called my daughter yesterday to tell her that I'd picked a zucchini. "Only one?" she asked. I went out to encourage the other blossoms. But I still don't believe I'll get too many z's. I haven't been that lucky.
(took place in 1991)   (written in 1992)

9. Presents and gifts.

Used here, "presents" refers to any action, trip, chore done willingly, or other intangible thing given to someone in honor of a special occasion; "gifts" means a particular *object*, a toaster or copy of a poem, given for the same reason.

Think back to the first gift you remember receiving. How old were you? Did you expect that particular gift? How did you feel immediately after you saw it? Do you still have the item? How long did you keep it? Was it something precious to you, or just another thing? Did anything happen to it along the way? Did you give it to your child?

As with former subjects, once you begin writing about this, other stories will suggest themselves. Keep jotting reminders onto your HIP, and write one or two of these before you finish for the day. How many stories surrounding this gift do your children know? Why don't they know more? What do you think of this gift now?

You may want to make a list of all the early gifts and presents you can remember, first, before you begin to write about them one at a time. If not, when you have finished writing about your first item, think of another gift or present that was significant in your life, something you remember clearly, think about sometimes, or still have in your possession. Who did you get it from? Why did they give it to you?

Gift:

On the top shelf of my closet, in the center where I can see her, sits the first bought doll I ever had. It was a birthday gift from my godmother. I had no idea it was coming, since none of us had bought dolls, and this was obviously a very special doll. Being a good Catholic child, I named her "Mary". She had a pale blue dotted-Swiss pinafore and hat on, with quarter-inch rick-rack trim on both, and white silky ribbed socks. I don't remember her shoes—just the black Mary Janes I made for her later out of a piece of oil-cloth. Her eyes closed when she lay down. I found that wondrous. Her head had molded reddish hair painted on. She was so beautiful. Now she wears a cream and blue sweater-booties-hat set that my mother had knitted for me before I was born, and which was accidently shrunk in the wash. When I look at the doll, I remember that all the lights were out except the kitchen and porch light the evening of my birthday in the house in Regina when Auntie Kay came over in her dark fur coat, her hair curled back in big rolls, and handed me the large box. I wasn't sure what to do with a "real" doll—whether one was allowed to actually play with

her or not. But she has stayed with me all these years, and I still say "hi!" to her once in a while when I walk through the closet.
Present:

One "present" I remember was when my parents took all of us adult children and spouses to see "Fiddler on the Roof" with Topol as "Tevye". According to my father, the part of Russia that "Fiddler" was supposed to have taken place, was close to where his family lived after they left Alsace-Lorraine. We had been told much of the history, and given books and pamphlets that my parents got from the AHSGR (American Historical Society of Germans from Russia), some even showing the plot of land my great-grandparents farmed in Katherinental. I have since seen "Fiddler" several times, play the music from it on the piano, and remember how special it was to receive the gift of a seeing that play.

You may remember plays, vacations, days of leisure—or single acts that were given to you as presents. Giving a service as a gift was common when I grew up and passed that along to my children. Did your family give intangibles for gifts? Tell about it. How did that get started? Why do they or don't they give "presents" as gifts?

10. Describing persons.

The major difference between describing persons, as opposed to things or places, is that people have feelings, and most of them do not want to hear negative things about themselves. On the other hand, if you are going to write openly and honestly, you cannot 1) lie:

"Joe was so wonderful every minute of our lives!" 2) ignore the truth: "That scar on my face—it just happened." 3) tell only part of the truth: "We were just talking. Then after I got out of the hospital....".

I'm not recommending you "dis" anyone or only talk about negative things. Think of it this way: we are all human and do things we wish we hadn't. But the fact is, we *did* those things. Suppose your father beat you with a leather riding crop until you bled; he may or may not regret it, but there are different ways to talk about it.

Example 1: That SOB hated me and ought to go to hell

Example 2: My father was a great disciplinarian

Example 3: He beat me with a riding crop until I bled.

The first example is emotional (as well you might be, given the circumstances), but it mixes up the *telling* of the incident with a *judgement* (SOB). It is best to tell what happened in factual terms without using inflammatory or judgemental language. Then at the end, if you have an opinion on the subject, state it. **Don't give the impression that your analysis and the facts are necessarily the same thing.**

In this situation, example #2 is ridiculous. Either you are still under his influence, fear his reprisals, or are too immature and naïve to see what was going on. No one should be beaten for any reason. You did not deserve that.

The factual truth is #3. "This is what happened,

and then I bled as a result." Those are all provable verities (or were at the time). Nothing in that statement is a judgement upon your father—it is only what he himself truly did.

So when you write of people who hurt you and of how they did so, write only (and all of) the **facts**. You do not need to show your writing to that person, if you have any reason not to. That person will not be hurt by what stays in your journal. And that person will not be *hurt* by the truth. He experiences some *pain* because of it (if you discuss it with him or tell someone else or he goes to jail), but he will not be *hurt*—he will have a chance to grow. You felt *pain* because of the beating, but the real *hurt* was done because your father thought you were so awful or bad that you needed beating and because he made you agree with his opinion of you. Didn't you? Isn't that why you hesitate to talk about it even now?

EXAMPLE OF FACTUAL NARRATIVE: My father beat me with a riding crop several times a week. Anything would set him off, mostly after he'd been drinking. He even had to replace a couple of crops that he wrecked after he "borrowed" them from the stables where he worked.

I would get into a curled–up position down on the ground once he got started, so only my back got bloody. Most of the time my shirt got ripped. The beatings would last until his arm got tired or his anger was lessened. After a while I didn't even scream.

EXAMPLE OF ANALYSIS/OPINION: I was very frightened of my father until I got old enough to realize that I could run away and survive on my own. I was afraid to criticize him at the time, but I see now how out of control he was. It took years for me to build up any self-esteem because of the way he treated me. I know now that he had no right to treat me like that--I wish I had known it then. It took a long time for me to live in reality all of the time, because I had trained myself to go somewhere else inside my mind while I was being beaten. I am angry that my father did all those things to me and now he is dead and I can't even yell at him. I yelled at a picture of him though. This whole thing has messed up a lot of my life, but I am going to take care of myself, continue with my therapy, and never treat my children like that.

It is not necessary to give an example of what a paragraph would be like with facts, judgements, and obscenities all mixed together. Trust me, it would not be as readable in years to come, nor would it touch the reader as much as if you wrote what actually happened followed by how you felt about it then and now.

I stand by my earlier statement that you should feel free to write about anything and any place and anybody.

This has been enough of a list for you to see that everything is grist for the mill. If you have read this far, tried out every exercise and suggestion, and still don't have any ideas of what to write, read a few more autobiographies. You will find that what those authors found important enough to write about were the everyday things, not only the rare tremendous experience.

As a rule, beginning Heritage writers (women more than men) tend to write about their families instead of themselves. They consider their lives so bound up with that of their partner and/or children and/or siblings and parents, that it is difficult for them to think of themselves, their own lives, as being of singular value.

At first, Heritage Writing will prove not to be the experience that your children imagined it would be, even though they may have been saying for years, "Mom, you ought to write your autobiography." When Mom actually does begin to write it, the children are usually surprised, having not thought of "Mom" as someone with a personal life in the first place. They may be shocked to read that she had all the fears and sex drive and silliness of any teenager in her youth.

It takes some people longer than others to reach the truth in their autobiographical writings. In the beginning, everything on their page will give the impression that life was perfect—all roses and a picket fence. If pressed, the writer may admit that life was occasionally less than that, but he or she will still find it hard to write about actual incidents and persons and feelings with the same degree of openness they will get to two or three years down the road.

Teachers who work with adults processing their memory–stories say that one of the greatest stumbling blocks for new Heritage memory–collectors is the worry that, because of their writing, someone may think badly of their family or one of its members. Parts of stories are left out, the endings changed, or the story is not told at all because of a misplaced sense of loyalty. It takes a while to accept that we are not responsible for other people's feelings. What opinion they form after they read the truth is not your doing. We are each responsible for ourselves.

It is also a fact that people in a class are more interested in their own writings than in the fact that you confessed one of your husband's faults in one of yours. Besides, sharing in every writing class or group I've ever been in or taught has always been optional. (More on sharing in **Chapter 23: Sharing, Groups, and Critique**.)

If you are going to go through the effort to do any Heritage Writings, do it right. Make it a collection of *true* stories that you will be proud of.

11. Memory–joggers

The following words are Memory–joggers. You can use them, or make your own list of words to remind you of things you would like to write about in the future. Just take a dictionary or spelling dictionary and browse through it, writing down words that catch your eye. You don't have to look at every page, just here and there.

As you read the list of words, circle or copy one or two that evoke particularly strong memories. Then write about them using whatever form you wish—personal essay, poetry, related lists, freewrite, etc., and put the results in your ABC file, using titles and crossreferences on your index pages.

Using newspapers, magazines, and other books in this way has the disadvantage that you may get hooked on the story and spend your writing time, reading. That's easy to do. Also, you won't find the variety of words there that you'll see in dictionaries.

This is the list of words:

airplanes	communicate	freedom
alcohol	company	funeral
allergy	computer	games
anger	crochet	garden
arguments	dance	gerbil
asbestos	death	grief
at peace	depression	guns
authority	dinner	gypsies
barn	dive	hair
barrel	doctors	
bats	dog	happening
beach	drawing	health
best friend	dreams	heaven
Bible	dresses	hell
black	driving	
blue	earthquake	hero
books	embroider	
brooder house	endless	honey
brothers	escalator	hoop
candlewicking	estate	hospitals
car accident	fairy tales	house
career	fakery	how I got here
carnival	fall	illness
cars	farm	in love
ceremonies	father	inherit
child	fear	injustice
chorus	feeling sick	joy
Christmas	fence	judgement
church	Ferris wheel	kitten
clay	fields	knife
clothes	fish	knit
cocktail parties	flowers	letters
coffee	fortune	

lightning
limousine
lingerie
lion
lunch
marriage
math
maturity
menu
military
miscarriage
misery
mother
music
my own space
near-death experience
night
nine
noise
nuns
nuts
ocean
officer
Olympics
opera
paint
payback
peace
pennant
perfect
persimmon
personnel
piano
pigs
planet
play
poetry
politics
pollen
practical jokes
priest
provoke
psychic
psychologist
purple
quilt
radio
radish
railroad
rain
raps
regrets
retreat
revelation
ring
risque
rite
room
sacraments
sad
sand
saxophone
scalp
school
seance
self-esteem
separation
sex
shell
ship
shoes
silence
sisters
slug
snacks
spats
spectacles
spectograph
spider
sports
spring
square
stories
storm
story
sublet
summer
sunburn
sunshine
swimming
talent
tans
teachers
tennis
therapy

sunshine
swimming
talent
tans
teachers
tennis
therapy
thunder
tidal wave
tombstone
toys
travel
tuxedo
TV
twelve
twenty
vampire
van
vanished
very happy
victory
volcano
volunteer
wants/needs
war
weather
weather vane
weight
white
wigs
wind
wingtips
winter

woodworking
work
worlds
wound
writing
yard sale
yarn

Making lists like this is good practice in word association. Start with the word "night" and write four other words that that reminds you of. Take one of those four and write four more about that, etc., till you run out of ideas. Then start with a whole new word, like "religion".

Some words on the list are homophonic, that is, they sound the same, but can have two meanings. Like "wind"--do we mean blowing air, or tidying up loose string? It's your choice. Use whichever meaning helps remind you of stories.

Chapter 20: Using Your Feelings, Emotions

One thing about youth today (which was especially noticeable as I taught a young male offenders' group) is that they have little hesitation in talking about their feelings. The step before that, which would be admirable in itself, is that *they know what feelings are.*

I told them that they are fortunate to know what feelings are; that it is wonderful they are able and willing to express them—not only the violent ones. I said it took some of my generation till they were 45 before they reached that stage.

The youths understood that by complimenting them I was not condoning the crimes by which they merited detention, nor was I saying that they had turned out perfectly since they'd had counseling there. It was just about one thing: FEELINGS. They seemed surprised when I told them that as a rule, generations back, no one thought much of his or her own feelings or recognized what role they played in life.

But this is a different generation.

I was describing what my grandmother wore in the early days. "She wore several petticoats, one on top of the other," I said. "I know because once when I was little and stayed overnight, I peeked through my fingers and watched her undress. After she had taken off her outer skirt and a couple of white petticoats, but still had at least one on, she saw me looking and came over to my bed to scold me."

"Why?" "For what?" they asked.

"For looking. In those days you weren't supposed to speak of or show your body to anyone," I said. "In fact, some religions and cultures even insisted that you bathe with some of your clothes on."

The boys stared with their mouths open. "You're kidding!" they said.

You may get the same reaction in a few years when you tell about your life now, and find that things have changed so much that it is difficult for another generation to think what we had is even possible.

When we spoke of statistical journal entries, these young men had difficulty comprehending writing without statement of feelings. I read them a couple days' worth of samples. They still did not quite understand that emotionless entries could stand on their own. I was secretly pleased that they were in such tune with their feelings.

For my best example, I told them how much my mother respected and revered the pope. How she and Dad went to church every day, and prayed the rosary, and did all those things the pope said to. But the day when the pope died, Mom wrote in her journal: 'The Pope died today. I scraped the windowsills in the den in preparation for painting.' And that was all." They were silent a moment and just looked at me.

At that moment I understood more of how my mother felt when she wrote that entry: "This is what happened. We can't do anything about it, so we might as well go on with the rest of our lives, even if we can't quite do much except a little window-scraping."

She never said she felt distraught. She didn't mention that she or Dad cried, yet I know that they must have been extremely upset. I don't know if they even talked about it together. She didn't say, "I'm upset," but it was implied in the juxtaposition of her two statements for that day. Until I began taking apart reasons for using feelings, and why or how people have lived without admitting they had any, I wasn't able to decipher her code for "I'm upset".

I don't think I am reading into what she said. I've come to this conclusion from knowing her, how she thought and spoke, and from the missing feelings in nearly all of her entries. In fact, the only time she poured out her heart on paper was right after Dad died. I had given her a blank book and encouraged her to write letters to Dad, telling him how she felt about his leaving. She did, and I read the book after she died. It was very special.

It is not unusual for people (especially men) to go to therapy and discover that they do not know what feelings are. Gathering knowledge about feelings is not a condemnation of what we did not know—it is a *learning experience*. "I feel that you are cheating me" is not a feeling; it is a thought. How does the cheating make you *feel*? Angry? Discouraged? Suspicious? *Those* are feelings. It helps to write down a list of feelings and look at it every once in a while. If you can use one of the words off the list, you are probably talking about feelings:

abandoned
abhor
admire
afraid
aghast
agitated
agony
alienated
am fond of
ambivalent
amused
angry
anguish
annoyed
annoyed
anxious
anxious
apprehensive
assured
astounded
attached to
attracted to
beaten
betrayed
bewildered
bewitched
bitter
blissful
bored
bothered
bugged
burdened
calm

can't stand
captivated
care for
certain
cheerful
cherish
comfortable
composed
confident
confused
confused
confused
contented
cool
debased
defiant
dejected
delighted
depressed
deserted
desire
desolate
despair
desperate
despise
despondent
detached
detest
disappointed
disconcerted
discontented
discouraged

disgraced
disgruntled
disgust
disheartened
dislike
disquieted
dissatisfied
distraught
distraught
disturbed
doubtful
down
downcast
drained
dread
dreary
dubious
easy
ecstatic
elated
embarrassed
empassioned
enchanted
encouraged
endangered
enraged
enraptured
entranced
estranged
exasperated
excitement
exhausted

expectant
fascinated
fatigued
fear
feel tenderly
toward
finished
flustered
flustered
flustered
forsaken
frazzled
fretful
furious
fury
galled
glad
gleeful
gratified
grief
griped
happy
harassed
hate
haunted
have a fancy
for
heartened
hesitant
high
hope
hopeless

horrified
humbled
hurt
impatient
impressed
incensed
indignant
ineffective
infatuated
inflamed
infuriated
insecure
inspired
insulted
intimidated
intoxicated
intrigued
invigorated
involved
irked
irritable
irritated
joyful
left out
like
loathe
lonely
lost
love
mad
merry
mind

miserable
mortified
nauseated
nonchalant
nonplussed
offended
optimistic
outraged
overcome
overjoyed
pain
perturbed
piqued
pissed
pleased
prize
provoked
put out
put down
regard
regret
relieved
resentful
resistant
restless
satisfied
scared
secure
see red
self-confident
serene
shame

shocked
shy
sick of
slighted
small
sorrow
sorry
spite
stimulated
stirred up
stricken
stung
stunned
suspicious
taken by
threatened
thrilled
tickled
timid
tired of
tired
took tortured
touched
trepidatious
troubled
uncertain
uneasy
uninterested
unloved
unsafe
unsettled
unsure

used up
useless
vexed
warmed
wary
weak
weary
worn out
worried
worthless
wretched
yearn

Chapter 21: Guidelines for Writing

Since the important part of Heritage Writing is *what you are saying,* not how you say it, "Guidelines" as discussed here will not include spelling, handwriting, or grammar. If you are interested in those things, see **Chapter 29: Writing Stories to Sell.**

These, however, are important to your story:
1. Length of the story: Not how long or short the story is, but whether you are padding it, dragging it on after it is over, repeating yourself. Just tell the story as it was.
2. Interest: Almost anything anyone would write about their personal life, especially their growing–up years, would seem interesting to me. What would make me put the book down would be if they had a lot of unexplained technical jargon, if their scientific or academic theories were worked out in the midst of their memories, if they wanted posterity to see that they really do understand the obscure corners of physics. For Heritage Writing, stick to the *memories* of your life. You can

write your theories and proofs and your philosophy in another volume.

3. Words used in telling: If you happen to be making a booklet for grandchildren of a few of your stories, keep it simple. Bear in mind the attention span and word-comprehension level of the children. Which is not to say you cannot use any words that are new to them. Just don't use too many, and explain what you do use. Children grow up quickly, so gearing the stories *only* to first grade reading level may limit the stories' popularity. Something like a story a middle-grade student would *listen to*, is best. I like to reread the fairy tales we read to our children all through grade school, but if they were written in very elementary words, I doubt you'd see me read any of them over again as an adult.

4. Content: If you are doing a book for a particular age group only, choose story lines that will make them feel happy they listened. Choose stories with content they can relate to. A pre-schooler might be interested in how you learned to tie your shoes, if you were one of those kids who always had a shoe missing when it was time to go someplace, your experience with new foods or with anything low to the ground, how you overcame your fear of the swimming pool, etc. I know you would not give a small child the burden of detailed abuse stories (unless he/she is in the same situation, and then only with very special treatment and the advice of a therapist), or a story that shows only the negative side of their grandparents. Tell that side, yes, but not now, not here. We are talking the usual grandparents here, not people who are a danger to their grandchildren. Tell what is *appropriate* if you are making a collection for a specific child or children.

You can tell *all* in your ABC Heritage Writing notebook.

5. And more: Natalie Goldberg, author of *Writing Down the Bones* (see Bibliography) has straight-out words for writers who want to know how to do it. She says to **keep writing no matter what.** Remember the part about not judging your work? Ms. Goldberg calls that keeping the creator hand moving so that the editor hand can't catch up with it.

Losing control when you write is preferable, she says. It is the key to authenticity.

Don't waste time and energy by saying things twice, like: "My new <u>car</u> which was a <u>Cadillac</u>." "My new Cadillac" will do.

Use specific words that show what clothes you wore and the name of the town or cafe, what colors things were, and what the weather was like. Wherever you can narrow it down and give the reader a clearer picture, do so. Writing "in general" is boring to the writer and the reader.

"Don't think," says author Goldberg. None of this starting to write and then second-guessing what you're talking about. Just get in there and write without looking back.

Natalie Goldberg is an excellent, internationally known writer, yet she says that when we are writing, we should **not worry about spelling or grammar. You are free to write the best or the worst stuff** in the universe, she says. **Seek the energy**—if something is scary, write about it. Bland, boring writing often avoids the truth.

Don't spend all your allotted time trying to figure out what you want to say—**start writing and figure it out as you go along.** You don't have to *keep* every single word you wrote, but it is guaranteed that you will write better and get at more truths this way than if you write a detailed outline first.

Does that mean I can't *cluster*? Of course not. Clustering (*Writing the Natural Way*) isn't outlining or figuring out all the words. **It is a way of not letting anything get lost.** Suppose I decided to write a story about rollerskating (as we used to call it). Which reminds me of several other things I might forget while I am writing the first story. So I cluster like this:

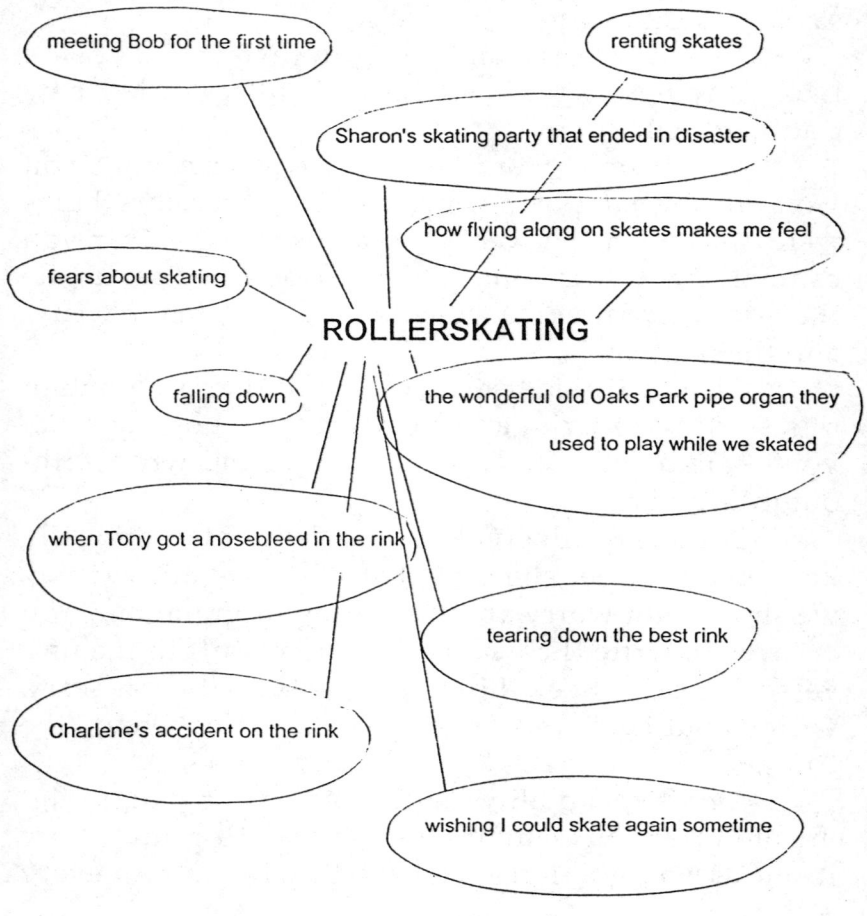

- meeting Bob for the first time
- renting skates
- Sharon's skating party that ended in disaster
- how flying along on skates makes me feel
- fears about skating

ROLLERSKATING

- falling down
- the wonderful old Oaks Park pipe organ they used to play while we skated
- when Tony got a nosebleed in the rink
- tearing down the best rink
- Charlene's accident on the rink
- wishing I could skate again sometime

Chapter 22: Variations on your POV

Most of us are opinionated about at least a few things. We've used a great deal of effort to educate our selves and learn about life in many ways. So when we come to a perfectly logical conclusion and someone disagrees with us, we are taken aback and have to either argue, or rethink our position. It is good practice, now that we are looking at the past anew, to look at certain disturbing or irritating memories from *several* points of view. How can we do that? Here is an example:

It was raining hard one rainy Sunday evening with all of us squished in the car on our way home from a drive when Dad decided to visit the Ks in Parkrose, a northern suburb of Portland. The usual streets to their houses were blocked off with barricades, and there were huge puddle–lakes standing on the road. My father took us home to Lambert Street and drove back to Parkrose where he loaded Uncle Max, Aunt Alina, Eva, Peter, and the twins into the car, along with some of their belongings into the car. They lived with us for about six months while the flood crested, receded, and they were able to clean out their house enough to live in it. They had been growing green onions commercially, probably some other things, too, but the onions are what I remember helping harvest, standing in knee-deep water before the flood got its highest.

My impression of the entire time they were with us, from the POV of an eight year old child was that the whole thing was a lot of extra work, and our house was extremely crowded. Things that were ours, we kids didn't want to share on that constant a basis. When Alina and Max yelled at each other, it scared us, because we'd never seen adults outside of our own family disagree so loudly. Their family's way of eating, sleeping, and living, was disruptive to ours, the ways *we* were used to.

When Eva, a teenager by then, taught me some songs like "Bye, Bye, Blackbird" and "Baby Face" off her sheetmusic, that was a new experience for me. The popular love songs of the day weren't things I knew something about, and sheet music was unheard of in our house, both because of the cost and because it was so secular. So Eva and I would go out in the field beside the house and she'd get me to memorize the words. I enjoyed that. It was a sort of borderline rebellion, the strongest I'd ever mounted to date.

The boys were having another problem The visitors brought play guns into the house, as well as adventure comics with violence and women with cleavage. We'd never seen anything like that and were forbidden to look at them, but sooner or later we each made the rounds of reading every single one. There was a lot of fighting and hairpulling among the kids, and a great disappoint for Ashley, who had been told there was someone her age (three) to play with, but that person only wanted to play with Bly.

That is my POV, or was as a child, my memory of that time. Suppose with what I know of my parents, I would try to tell the story from their points of view. Why? To broaden my mind. To see if any other points of view make sense to me. To see if it would answer any questions that remain in my mind, or explain why some things were the way they were.

Not just, "Oh, yeah, I thought about it this way and they thought about it that way. I get it." Let's go deeper. Let's get into their minds, feel what they felt. Give it a try.

POV of my mother:

We are all in the car on our way home. It has been louder earlier with the kids arguing over who sits where or who's poking whom. (Days before seatbelts, kids moved around a lot) Now the younger kids are falling asleep. It is getting so dark and the rain is coming down so hard, that it is hard to see the road, especially here on the outskirts of town. All of a sudden we see the barricade. "I'd heard there were floods out here," says John, "But I didn't think they had gotten that far." We stop and talk to a policeman at the barricades. He absolutely refuses to let us by, says they are evacuating everyone beyond the barricades anyway. That's when John decides to take us home to empty the car and get beds ready while he goes to pick up the Ks. What he actually does is make a few more trips after that to get whatever furniture and pictures and clothes he can pack into the car and Max's truck. The girls are sleepy and don't want to help get out the extra blankets. We make some beds on the floor by pulling the mattresses off. Some of us sleep on the box spring and bed frame, others on the floor. There isn't much room to walk, even in our bedroom which Alina and Max will share with us. We also have only one bathroom in the house. But what are you going to do? They're relatives who can't afford a motel. Besides, who knows how long this will last. Maybe the river will crest tonight and they'll be back home in a couple of days. John said it would be shameful to let relatives go to public housing when we have enough room for them here.

Later: The kids are constantly fighting over our kids' toys, over their kids' things, over everything. Max and Alina want Marie to go along and help save the onion crop, so I get left babysitting for everybody else. Well, it can't be helped.

Much later: I didn't think we'd get through as many months as we did. Alina and I raise kids differently and have so many differences of opinion about other things. Sometimes I get so angry! The house seems so small these days. I am losing my energy cooking for so many people and trying to get the usual things done. We're told in church not to complain and love our neighbor, but it's so hard. John is lucky—he gets to leave the house and go to work some hours of the day. But I am in the middle of it from morning till late at night.

Remember, this is a projected POV, not what my mother would actually write or share with anyone, since it was her custom not to discuss feelings on paper. But I am almost certain she was feeling these things.

Now for the projected POV of the adult male guest, Uncle Max:

Just when we're getting our garden business going, right before the onion harvest this has to happen. We're losing everything except what we hauled to John's. Several houses near ours have floated away already. Ours is still standing in the water. We drive by every couple of days to the hilltop and look with binoculars to check it out. I have to get out of the house—not being able to work is driving me nuts. The kids do nothing but fight, and Alina and Barbara disagree about a lot of things, too. This has gone on too long for all of us. It will take a couple of months to get the mud out of the house and make it good enough to live in—if that's possible. A lot of work. Peter's only 9, Eva works after school, and the little kids aren't any help. Can't afford to hire it done. It's very upsetting. The government hasn't decided if we get any aid yet. Alina says I yell at her too much, but what'd you expect? I've got a lot of things on my mind.

Lastly, see if your own original point of view has changed because of any insights you received as you wrote the stream–of–consciousness points of view of other persons involved. Is there anything you would like to add to what you first wrote?

It was probably at least as hard on the Ks as it was on us. I used to think, charity is one thing, but this is going too far. It was almost more than we all could handle. Looking back, it was the right thing to do, and I'm glad my parents were generous enough to do it. I wish all the kids had had some psychological preparation, though.

Afterwards it seemed strange going to visit the Ks after they moved to another house (theirs was totalled). It was like we knew each other's intimate secrets (strange for that time) like who snored or what they argued about in bed and now we were acting polite to each other: "Yes, I'll have a cookie. No more lemonade for me, thanks." I remember on our first visit looking over at Aunt Alina and seeing that she was studying me.

"How are you doing, then?" she asked. Practically nobody spoke to kids.

I wondered, with all she now knew about me, how far in depth she expected me to answer. "What do you mean?" I said.

"How's it going for you?"

I hesitated. "Fine," I said, as I would have to a stranger. I didn't know what else to say.

HAVING WRITTEN

VI. WHERE TO GO FROM HERE

Chapter 23: Sharing, Groups, and Critique

The purpose of sharing is to give you ideas and encouragement, not to make you feel so inadequate that you never want to write again. Sharing and critique are *arts*, to be learned by the rules first.

1. Groups: Joining or founding

As has been mentioned before, almost every town has writers' groups, both for memory writing and for professional critique. If your town does not have the type of group you need, and you would like to share and discuss the writing of your Heritage Memories, start a group of your own. Print an ad in a local paper and see if anyone is interested. If you get no response that way, ask your neighbors and friends directly. Often people read notices or advertisements and say to themselves that that really sounds interesting, and that they ought to do something about it. But they put it off and never really do unless someone like you approaches them face to face or over the phone.

It is also possible to discuss by e-mail over the computer, or by regular mail, depending on how much you have to share at one time.

2. Rules for the Group
    a. Necessity of

You don't *have* to do Heritage Writing with partners, but like everything else, sometimes it is more fun that way. There are times in life for suggestions, and times when only rules will do: this is one of the latter. If you have decided to join or found a group, set up the ground rules first. Having been in critique groups that failed and ones that functioned efficiently, I can assure you that this is vital for the smooth, natural functioning of the group. The longer your group works together, the more you all will realize how having an agreed-upon structure frees you.

    b. Group Structure

These are good rules:

    1. Decide on a **maximum number of participants**. 5-10 works well. Each person must be serious about showing up each time (except for rare problems), or give up his or her place in the group.

    2. Agree on a **regular meeting time and place**, not more than twice a month, unless you are all retired, or have enough time so that no one in the group is unduly burdened by getting writings ready weekly. As to place, some libraries offer public meeting rooms, as do

some public buildings, such as banks and real estate companies. One writer's group I know of meets over lunch, although it would be my preference to keep food and writing separate.

3. Talk about **leadership**. Do you want one person to be in charge for a number of months, or a year? Would you like to try rotating leadership each meeting? See what works out best for each of you. And yes, elected leadership is important. You know very well that if there is no designated leader, someone will emerge from the group and be its unofficial leader forever. Is that what you all of you want?

4. Decide on the **focus of the group**. Are you writing for yourselves, your children, nameless posterity, for sale? You may change goals with each piece you write, but the type of critique you engage in should match those goals. Do not comment on spelling or grammar, or even tease about that if your group is for Heritage Writing only. There should be agreement among you about critique before you procede. These discussions about structure are foreshadowings of how smoothly your group will function.

5. The **procedure for critiquing and sharing** should be agreed upon, also. One that works well is:

a. Divide the time among those who are there. If you have two hours and eight people are sharing, each person will be allotted 15 minutes. Assign a timekeeper each time and stick to the agreement rigidly. In the case of where someone has a long piece, several pages, the writer will have to decide which aspect of discussion will fit into his/her 15 minutes. Writers with short pieces have the prerogative of giving away some of their time to a person with a long piece, but they don't have to. Sometimes a four-line poem takes longer to discuss than an essay. It is each person's choice.

 b. When it is your turn, you decide how you wish to use the time. You may just talk about how you came to write these things, and read some of them to the group. Or not read them. Or discuss some things related to Heritage Writing. Or hand out copies for others to read, leaving time for comments. It is *your* time.

 c. **Giving critique**: While the critique or comments are being given, the person whose work is being discussed says nothing, but takes notes on a piece of paper, so that when the critique is finished, or when time for that person is about to run out, he or she can answer questions that were raised, explain anything that needed explaining (bear in mind that if they don't "get" what you're trying to say, probably your progeny won't, either) and thank the group for the comments.

  When you are doing the critiquing, DO NOT ever attack *anyone* or *what they write*. You are not allowed to cross swords on their opinion or point of view. The critiquing should match what they have asked for.

 For example, Joe has two short pieces, copies of which he hands out to everyone. He says, "I am going to read one of these out loud, and let you read the other one to yourselves. What I would like to know is, are the pieces clear enough? Do you understand the incident I am trying to explain?"

 d. **Receiving critique**: After the pieces are read, there is a lively discussion as to clarity—two writers think the first piece is obscure, but the rest do not. They all agree on the second piece, that they understand it very well. Joe takes notes, especially the two dissenters' reasons for thinking the piece needs clarification. He asks them how they would do it.

Once the clarification issue is over, the writers may volunteer other things, like asking if Joe ever thought of putting these two writings in a series of similar writings, or like commenting favorably on some word or phrase or way of looking at something.

e. Potentially negative comments (after all, what can be truly negative about writing the way you want to?) should be couched in questions, like the other remarks—but very gentle questions. For instance: "I have a problem with the cartoon you drew alongside your article. It seems to give a different slant from the writing. Am I missing something here?" Then Joe can explain, or write down the comment for future revision.

The point of the critique is the writing, not the point of view. The best and easiest way is to frame everything in a question. Supposing someone had a typo: instead of reading "religion", the word read "region". Even though anybody could tell by the sentence that "religion" was the word that they meant. That would be more than a grammar problem—it might be a matter of the reader's not understanding the story. So you might say, "Did you mean to say 'region' on line 1, page 7? If you did, I don't understand what you mean to say there. Could you explain it, please?" NOT: "Hey, that word 'region' is s'posed to be 'religion'."

No matter what you say, your tone of voice, body language, and words must be respectful of the other person's work, even if you diametrically disagree with their opinion.

You will have to practice giving and receiving critique a number of times before it feels natural. You see, everyone's works are their baby, their own creation. You, the parent, hold it up for admiration (maybe a little suggestion here and there), but you're not expecting attack and you should not have to defend yourself in any way. That is why you are quiet while the critique persons are speaking. You decide what you wish to accept (use), and what you wish to merely listen to.

It is like a new dress you designed—as far as you are concerned, it is as perfect as you can make it. If someone says you are horrible or the design is horrible, that doesn't benefit anyone. But if someone asks, "Did you mean to have two buttons and three buttonholes here?" it is a graceful way for you to discover a place you may wish to change—but you don't have to change it, remember. Maybe you like it that way. So you say, "Thank you for the suggestion." Or: "I'll think that over." Then you do think it over and decide, yes, I'll add another button, or no, that looks just fine the way it is.

Persons who are giving the critique should not *give* it personally, either. If they did, their feelings would get hurt every time you didn't use one of their suggestions.

When the time for the group meeting is up, or better yet, for 15 minutes before the meeting, have a social time when you can get a drink of water or coffee/tea, or just visit in general. It will get that need to "catch up" with everybody out of the way so that personal things don't pop up during the critiquing. It will also get some rapport running which will make things function more smoothly during the meeting.

Peter Sears, a writer/poet and staff member of the Oregon Arts Commission, teaches that it's all right to edit journals, unless it's evident that you did. You should not refine them too much. It takes away the spontaneity. For editing suggestions, see **Chapter 29: Writing Stories to Sell.**

Critique in Heritage Writing is different from what playwrights get handed by critics of the major newspapers a few hours after opening night. The goal of their plays is to please the public (and therefore, make money). The goal of Heritage Writing is whatever goal you decide it is in handing down your story.

Chapter 24: About Genealogy

As was mentioned in the first chapter, **Heritage Writing** is not making family trees or doing research for our roots—it is recording our personal memories. However, since more than half the adults who have learned **Heritage Writing** from me have also done beginning or extensive work in genealogy, a few words on bridging the two may be helpful.

There are a certain number of "ready–made" stories about your family out there somewhere, and it may be useful for you to find them. We didn't just wake up one day and invent the concept of recording our stories—it has been around for a long time. Ask among your close and peripheral relatives to see if anyone has written his or her story, and see how they feel about sharing copies with you and your children.

Bear in mind that at some point, someone may ask you the same question: "Would you mind sharing copies of your memory–stories with [a potentially unlimited number of] my side of the family?" It is something you should start thinking about as soon as you have written enough to share.

I know that some of you have only just begun to be able to do the very public thing of writing down your thoughts at all, and to think of passing around copies may be too much at this time. But think about it. Share a little here and there (your decision as to which writings) with "safe" audiences. When you die, they're all going to see it anyway— that's why you wrote it, right? Share when you are ready. If you feel more comfortable saving the sharing until after you leave this earth, that's all right. These are your memories, it is entirely your choice, and no one has a right to grumble about it.

If you are not sure you *ever* want anyone to see your writings, and you are just experimenting with writing them down for now, arrange with someone you can absolutely trust to have them burned, sight unseen, should you die suddenly. Then you can relax and write safely.

If you are ambivalent about sharing, take some of the most uncontroversial stories and send some copies around as Christmas presents: "My gift to you— stories from your heritage." You may get such good feedback that you are encouraged to send more next year. Wouldn't you have loved to receive five or ten stories a year from your parents' POV of their childhood memories?

In the case of that relative—and we all have them—who sees his/her role as "straightening you out", telling you what *really* happened, or commenting unfavorably on your writing style, reread **Chapter 7: Dealing with relatives who remember incidents differently.** Be firm, but polite: "These are *my* memories. You are welcome to write your own, but you are not invited to criticize mine." When he/she realizes that you are not going to 1) get upset, 2) change your writing to *his/her* memory-stories, or 3) stay in the same room or on the phone with him or her if they are being negative, they will get the idea and leave you alone. That one- or two-relatives-per-clan who persist should be walked out on *immediately* and *every time* they begin to tirade. Better that you concentrate on friends you choose who give you joy than on irritating persons you stick with just because they are "blood".

The stories you are looking for may turn up from unexpected sources, from relatives you didn't even know you had, as with my great-uncle who wrote what turned out to be fifteen typewritten pages about life beginning in 1853 when his father was born in the village of Strassburg near Odessa on the Black Sea. My mother gave me the handwritten pages which I typed and copied, including several news clippings about him and his family, and his published obituary, and distributed in colored 9x12" envelopes to my children, parents, aunts and uncles, and siblings.

Uncle John was a man with foresight; he gave full **names, dates, marriage partners, cities and towns, listed siblings (including deceased), and described details** we could only guess at otherwise, e.g.,

In the years 1901 to 1903 German-speaking people from near the Black Sea in Southern Russia, settled here in Blumenfeld [between Sedley and Odessa, Saskatchewan, Canada] after being detained and deloused at Qu'Appelle, a stepping off point for immigrants. Here, during and after a period of quarantine

each family equipped themselves with a nucleus of soil-tilling implements, flour, and a few yard-goods before proceeding in a southerly direction, about twenty miles, to the land flowing with milk and honey.

It was toward the end of April, 1902, when the trek to the homesteads began. Each family had a wagon now loaded with plow and harrow, a tent, some things brought from the old country, food, and on top of all that the family of eight. The first few miles was heavy bush, the trail winding around sloughs creating the odd stuck that necessitated unloading and reloading. All this was fun for the younger boys but I fear Mother was beginning to wish she had never left the Old Country.

He had a natural sense of humor: In my mother's periodic count of noses she would often exclaim, "Where's John and Andrew?" We always turned up again with excuses that only mothers would believe.

Whatever year Uncle John wrote this, he was in tune with his childhood: Of course we would have exciting adventure stories: We saw a herd of antelope down by that bush, a fox, a wolf, and a digging animal that later came under the name of "badger". We were really going to like this country.

He mentions details of life then, that generations of today are probably not aware of: Father did the most important thing on the first or second day of squatting, that is to find the iron peg that designates one corner of the square one hundred and sixty acres of land, now home. It must have been a blessing and a thrill, and the beginning, in reality, of his dream that eventually all of his six boys would possess their own land. That would have been impossible in the country by the Black Sea.

He also mentions neighbors (first and last names), other acquaintances and relatives that settled in the same area, lists what was built first, and what part of the village was formed by the time the railroad came in, how far one place was from the next, and exactly how work was done without machines. This, incidentally gives us an insight into unfamiliar animals at the same time: **Oxen, the solid beasts of burden, did much of the heavy field work in the pioneer years.** A pair of them could pull a sulky plow or a disk–harrow with the same ease as three horses, but they were stubborn, they preferred their own gait––from *slow* to *very slow* and *stop*. Not just stop, but lie down; and once one lay down, what a time to get him up on all fours again! To just twist his tail was not enough, you would have to build a fire under him.

To begin with, oxen preferred to move slower than horses and liked to go in any direction except forward. This was both maddening and tiresome for the boy or man in charge. Swearing didn't help either. The use of a whip would help a little for a step or two. There was no danger of a team of oxen running away with you, with one exception: if they smelled water, a slough within a couple of hundred yards away they perked up, and come hell or high water you couldn't stop them from making for it and then lying down in it. Well, why not––it was refreshing.

Oxen had their good points, too. They were nice and friendly when in haying time they pulled a wagon-rack from haymow to haymow obediently since they could graze at every stop. After all, they were pioneering as well as the settlers, suffering along and having their

Dear Grandchildren,

I am so glad to know you love good music (even if you find it hard to practice at times, when you rather wish to play); Your Mama did too, but see how she plays now, and even played in Church. Someday you will find great enjoyment when you can play a nice organ, and sing, you never get lonely.

I am going to tell you what happened one evening, your Mama was playing the organ for a long time, it was a moonlight night; and I sat in the other room looking out into the snow, but to my surprise a little rabbit came right up to the window, sat there to listen how your Mama played, then he started to run around, following the little path in the garden around the whole square, sit down and listen some more, and so three times already; he got so funny jumbled as if in harmony with the music, I wonder if he liked music too? Do you think so?

Then one day Grandpa sat in the yard to play his accordion; all the horses were in the yard, they all did come closer, but the one (we called him Dan) he came and started to jump up and down, sometimes he was in the air with all four legs then when we laughed at his tricks he ran away, came back to do the same thing over and over again; we believed he liked the music.

Maybe you will have a chance to see the M.P. with their horses doing their musical rides; what I saw was very nice. Then we saw a man come with a big bear, he held him on a line when another man played a music box and the bear danced. So I believe the animals like music, only little Benny it hurt his ears to come close to it.

Hoping you will always like good music, practice it daily, then someday you will also play for

Your Grandma

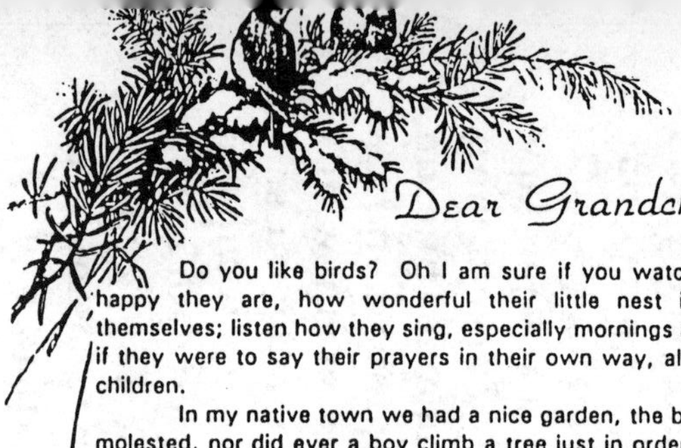

Dear Grandchildren,

Do you like birds? Oh I am sure if you watch and see how 'happy they are, how wonderful their little nest is, all built by themselves; listen how they sing, especially mornings and evenings as if they were to say their prayers in their own way, along with God's children.

In my native town we had a nice garden, the birds were never molested, nor did ever a boy climb a tree just in order to destroy the nest, only once a disobedient boy, he crawled up on the wall of the school, holding on to the plaster trimmings, it broke and he fell, hurting himself so badly that he died two days later. Our Teacher told us never to be so cruel to destroy a nest.

The swallows came and build their nests in our open veranda, we did watch them feed their young ones, it was all so nice.

Then we had the rose hedges in the garden, the little golden bird it was called the "Fence-King" it was his custom to slip in and out among the roses, looking for insects, and often playing hide and go seek in and out making a joyful note; it's a wonderful sight to see.

Then the meadow larks, and there were many sky larks, they sang so nice, and especially as they flew up in the air so high, and still singing their sweet notes.

Oh I wonder is and how many kinds of birds you have there where you live, and be sure to watch them, but never harm them, for God made them too.

God bless you and all children that love birds.

Your Grandma

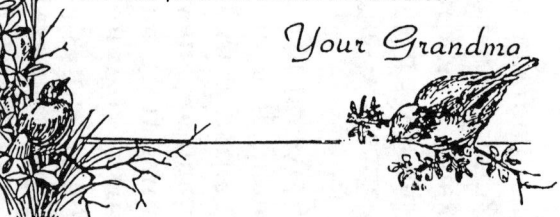

periods of leisure.

He writes personal notes about World War II, his second war: The voyage across the Atlantic was bloody awful. Our convoy consisted of three CPR ships carrying none but military units and equipment from across Canada. We embarked at Halifax. The Atlantic was rough, and being winter, we stayed below deck. After we saw the last of Canada—the coast of Newfoundland—the convoy headed east, then north and east zig-zagging continuously to avoid (they said) contact with German submarines. A German radio announcer who called himself Lord Haw-Haw was heard almost daily giving the approximate position of our ships. This frightened us knowing that enemy subs were all over the Atlantic. All the way across we had strong north winds causing the ships to pitch and roll so that in the dining areas, tables and chairs had to be chained to the floor, and most everyone got seasick.

As I write this page, my mother's cousin in Canada calls to request a copy of Uncle John's story to duplicate for relatives in her town—this "book" has been popular for 10 years already.

Let's get *your* story out there!

NOT:

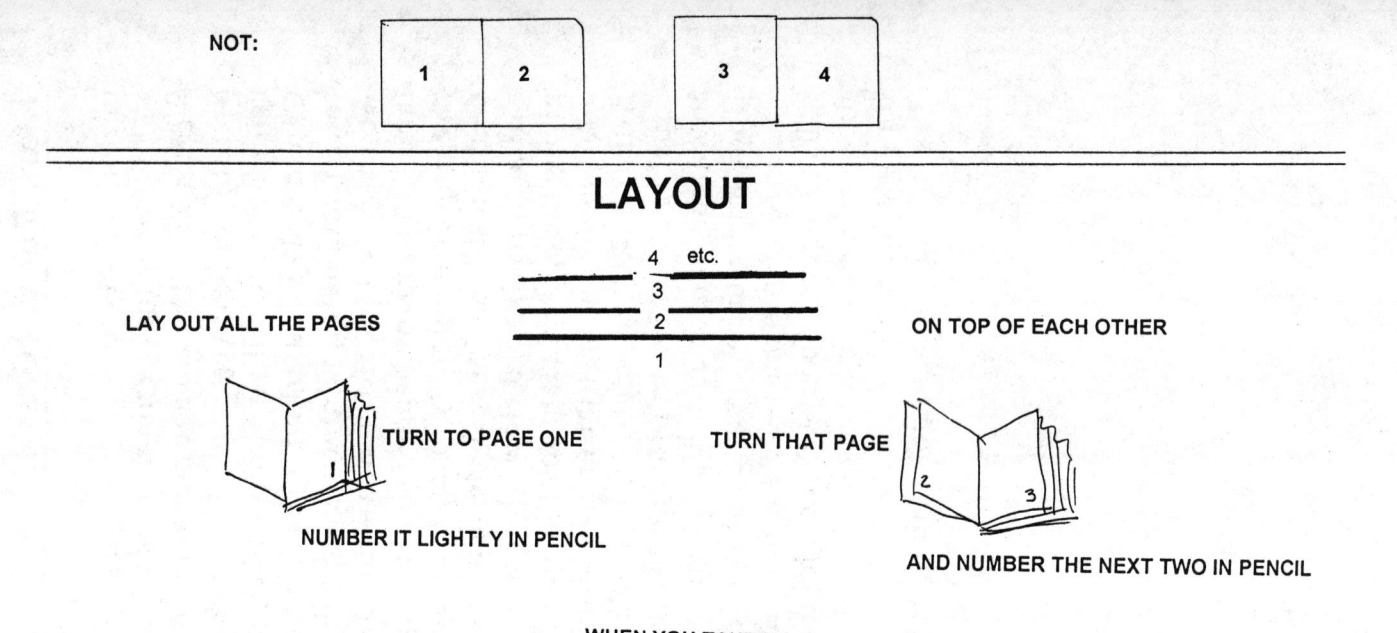

| 1 | 2 |
| 3 | 4 |

LAYOUT

LAY OUT ALL THE PAGES

TURN TO PAGE ONE

NUMBER IT LIGHTLY IN PENCIL

ON TOP OF EACH OTHER

TURN THAT PAGE

AND NUMBER THE NEXT TWO IN PENCIL

CONTINUE TURNING
AND NUMBERING PAGES
TILL YOU ARE FINISHED

WHEN YOU TAKE THE
STACK OF PAGES APART,
THEY WILL BE NUMBERED
LIKE THIS:

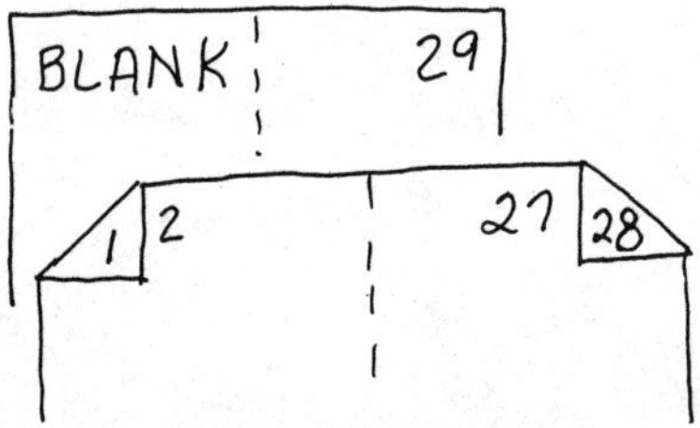

BLANK 29
1 2   27 28

AND SO ON.

Chapter 25: Adding drawings, photos

Audio tapes, home movies, video tapes, computer disk copies—the list is endless where you might get material besides your own to hand down to your children.

An easy (and inexpensive) way to collect a booklet of stories (others' or yours) is to type them on 8 1/2 x 11" paper in letter landscape form, two newspaper columns, leaving extra room in the center for the staple or binding. From clip art books (I find these of greater variety than computer clips), add illustrations, extending them here and there with *black* ink lines (ballpoint is okay). Be sure to plan the layout as to page numbers, depending on the final number of stories to be included.

If you are not yet computer fluent, an artist by trade, or in the printing business, this explanation will help: **letter landscape** refers to 8 1/2" x 11" typing paper that has been turned so that the longest side is horizontal.

Two newspaper columns means that if you use that computer setting, you will be able to write one column (side of the double-page) and then the next, as opposed to writing the first lines of each column, then the second lines of each, etc. See the example for an idea about text and clip art layouts.

A clip art book, available in office supply, stationery, novelty paper, and bookstores, is a stapled large workbook-sized collection of art all of one variety, e.g., one book may be all arrows and signs, another will be Victorian quasi-etchings, a third may be stained glass designs, etc. What you do is pick out a book (they cost little) and make copies of the pages you wish to cut and paste around your story. See each individual book for copyright information. Mostly, you can use anything as long as you don't sell the art as if it were your own work. When in doubt, write for permission (address inside book).

The layout of the pages means that a single sheet of paper, front and back, WILL NOT be stories 1, 2, 3, and 4. See example. Using half your page for each story, you can make a sample layout out of scratch paper. Say you have 29-30 stories. You would use 8 double-pages (8 sheets of 11 x 8_ paper, turned horizontally, numbered front and back.) Lay the pages on top of each other, folding them in half so that they look like a little unstapled book. Now start to number the pages in order: 1 for the first side, turn the page, 2 for the left side, 3 for the right side, turn the page, etc. When you are all finished, take the pages apart and look at the numbers. Surprise! But that is the order you will print them in if you want a consecutively numbered booklet.

Or, to make it simpler, type or write the story (with or without art) to fit one side of the page, leaving a full inch margin all around. Number the pages 1–2–3–etc. Now cut them up and paste the proper page across from its (printing) partner. Xerox the results.

If you don't care about the order of the stories, ignore all of this.

You might want to add another page (half in front of page 1 folded, and the other half after the last story) for a table of contents in front, or a personal note in the back. And one colored page (same size, same fold) for a cover. Use whichever format pleases you.

All original drawings should be in black ink in order to copy well.

A saddle–stapler or long–arm stapler that will reach nicely into the middle of your booklet might be available for loan at your library or neighborhood (or college) art center. After one set of books, I found it worthwhile to buy one from an office supply store.

Chapter 26: Copying, printing memory–stories

If you intend to do full–page black and white drawings, test them on a copy machine before you do the full run. Greys and other tones come through very well on modern black and white copiers. These machines can also enlarge and reduce several sizes at the touch of a button, for a nickel a page. (By the time this goes to press, who knows what wonders will be available!) Sketches and cross–hatched texture (as in the daily comics) print well on a standard copier. For special effects, you might want to check out graphics and illustration textures in an art supply shop.

A word about copiers. Check the window––if it copies with blotches or black streaks or dots, get it cleaned. Test one page for darkness level of print, and one for illustrations. Don't settle for a machine that is almost out of toner––ask to have a new cartridge put in. The work you are doing is too precious to do sloppily. You want these pages to last a long time and get a lot of reading. Smudges and faded print are unacceptable. Go to another store, if there is no choice.

On the other hand, if your local businessperson does an excellent job in copying and collating (some shops have collating machines behind the counter), compliment him or her, tell how pleased you are because this is important to you, and then return to that place the next time you need copying. A good, dependable copy outlet is invaluable.

Get bids from several outlets for your large print jobs. You will save $$$!

Chapter 27: Heritage Boxes and Games

A Heritage Box may be a raspberry-colored foot locker, an decorated cube-trunk, a homemade wooden box, or a large plastic lidded container of your favorite design. It also may be a ph-balanced set of containers for photos and papers, designed to keep your stories intact for a very long time—at least until you are finished paying for the ph-balance. No, that's not fair. Products designed to preserve heritage items are expensive, but not completely unaffordable to most people. They are available by catalog and in local outlets in most large cities—look in your Yellow Pages for a phone number. Compare products, claims, prices, guarantees, and company history / reputations before you buy.

My choice is the colored footlocker—something about the brass corners, the low shape, plenty of room, and choice of colors attracts me. One for each child is perfect for storing copies of everything Heritage, including photos. Every person who has gone through the trauma of having any of his or her siblings turn into unrecognizable vultures upon their parents' deaths, vows to construct a better system for the next generation. Nothing is foolproof, but duplicating the material with exactly the same Heritage material for each child will eliminate some of the problems.

Why not keep it in a cardboard box? Have you sniffed what paper stored in a cardboard box smells like after a couple of decades? Not great. Musty. You don't get the feeling you'd like to sit there and pore through the Heritage items unless you have to. Cardboard absorbs moisture and every other foul odor around it. A little extra money for wood or plastic is well worth it.

There are some "life" games out that are little more than throw the dice and move on. Some of the better games have cards and places to move and encourage the telling of past and present stories, but have what I call "waste–of–timers" like: *give the person on the left 3 taps on his bald spot*—which has nothing to do with collecting stories.

There are many varied–quality games with excellent blurbs in the catalogs—don't be fooled into buying any old thing. If you find a game that works well, get it. Then write me and tell me about it in care of this publisher. Because what I'd like to see wasn't available in a game, I made up my own: **"The Heritage Story Game."** It is the best game for use with this book because it supports the theories we've talked about, it is a non–threatening enjoyable way to jog your memory for stories, and is adjustable as to number of players and length of playing time. It can be played by younger or mature players, by families or adult friends. For information on purchasing **"The Heritage Story Game,"** see the back page of this book.

Chapter 28: Writing with your children

Of the many books I've gone through, the one with the most ideas for writing with your children, starting even before they can actually print anything, is *Kids Have All the Write Stuff* by Sharon A. Edwards and Robert W. Maloy. (See section **VII: Favorite Related Materials**.) My own children have been adults for years, and at the moment I have no grandchildren, but when I opened this book for the first time, I couldn't stop reading. It made me want to get home and try out some of this stuff myself. If you only buy one book about writing with/for kids, buy this one. It will not only increase your child's (and possibly your) communication skills, but it is great fun!

You may choose not to write with your children, but to read them stories you have written. Do whatever works out best for your family situation. As a parent who favors bedtime stories, you could try telling your child(ren) a short story or anecdote or description from your childhood. Make it a participatory game by encouraging your child to choose the subject matter (in the beginning, give him/her several options till they get used to the idea), like: Shoes, First Grade, Underwear, or Mud Puddles.

Example: **Mud Puddles (bicycle, Lambert Street, worms)**

I didn't know how to ride a bicycle when I little because we couldn't afford one till I was 10 years old. I had never heard of training wheels. My bike was *very* heavy––a used Schwinn. I tried to keep my balance on the gravel driveway and on the lawn till I could go a few feet without having to stop or fall over. The nearest pavement was a half mile away, the very busy 82nd Avenue, and they hadn't invented bike lanes yet. I tried riding on the rims of the deep potholes on the street in front of our house, but every time a car came by, it splashed water from the puddles onto the rest of the road, so it was always muddy out there. The deepest pothole in front of our house was shaped like Africa and went from our side of the street almost all the way across to the blackberry brambles. When we said "The Mud Hole", we meant that particular puddle.

One day after I had balanced myself on the Schwinn several times in a row, I thought I would show off for my father, so I waited out on the street for him to come home from work. Dad came out onto the porch, and I said, "Look at this!" I got on my bike and drove on the rims of the potholes down the street, got off my bike and turned it around, and drove back to our house. Just before I came to The Mud Hole, I took one hand off the handlebars and waved to my father. In a flash I was lying down in the yukky water with the heavy bike on top of me. My father was laughing and trying to seem sympathetic at the same time. I lifted up my arm and there were huge worms hanging from it! I screamed stuff like: "There's WORMS in here!" "Get that bike off me!" "Where's my shoe?" "Stop laughing!"

But it was funny to me, too, after I had had a bath and change of clothes.

You may want to tape your story (you'll get used to talking naturally with the recorder on, the more you do it) or at least mark a reminder on your HIP (Haphazard Index Page).

Some nights, *you* choose a category and let your child tell *you* a story which you tape and get typed up later for your child's ABC memory book. Or let your child type it for keyboard practice. Or hire it out to a typist when the tape is full, if you can afford it. As long as you remember that telling these stories, listening to them, and recording them for posterity is important.

Somehow, in showing your child the child you used to be, the soft vulnerable underside of this tall macho adult, the bonds between you are strengthened. Your child is less quick to consider you an alien having no part of his real life, when he/she gets to the teen years. Or, even if he/she acts foreign to his/her child–self, somewhere not–so– deep inside that teen, these stories and feelings live. When the hormone turmoil is over, the visible bonds will emerge, stronger than ever because you showed your child how much you care by spending this time telling stories, by sharing your own childhood secrets. Besides which, you have learned more on a deeper level about your child's inner self and because of this, may be able to better respond when "situations" arise later.

Another way of getting your child used to writing stories is by beginning with letters. Teach and encourage your child to write letters to grandparents (even if they live in the same town), to relatives, friends, their guardian angel, a favorite stuffed animal—or to you. When writing "thankyous" becomes a customary thing, can writing stories be far behind? Besides improving your child's communications skills, you are helping him/her grow, to make a habit of looking back to check out how things have affected his/her life, to learn by observation. This is the foundation of learning to make rational decisions.

As you teach your child(ren) to cherish and collect their own stories, show them ways of sharing the tales, e.g., printing them in booklets. With the proliferation of copy machines and computer software, as well as computer instruction in the schools, children are often more adept at this than we were 10 years ago. (Stress telling the truth, as opposed to spectacular exaggeration.) As a grandparent, would you not be thrilled to receive a little collection of your grandchild's stories—his/her view of life so far?

Chapter 29: Writing Stories to Sell

It is not necessary to *sell* your writing in order to get good feedback from it. Selling it does not make it worthwhile—it is worthwhile *first*, then you decide if you are going to edit and try to sell it.

If you have not written professionally before, and decide you would like to publish your stories (privately or through a publisher, both for general distribution), the best thing you can do for yourself is to take a good writing course, preferably from a local author who writes well (not just on popular subjects). Community colleges offer and know of courses like this. Do not be afraid to do this—you are going to be pleasantly surprised when you find out that: 1) the greater the author (*really* great, not just well-known), the kinder and more approachable he/she is; 2) nearly everyone in the class comes thinking they will surely be the "bottom of the group" in experience; 3) most writers are supportive and give good suggestions; and 4) you will look forward to your "class night".

Remember that you are writing to *touch* others, not to impress them.

Also see section **VII: Favorite Related Materials.**

Chapter 30: Last Words

What is the best time of the day to write? Where is the best place to write? As with exercising (but having a lot more fun), the answer is: When and where you will do it. If you are a night person, write while others sleep. Sometimes at three in the morning, if I happen to wake up enough to get my brain going, it starts telling me stories that I know I have to write down, so I go to my computer and do it; then I can sleep.

When you write doesn't have to be the same time every day, but if you plan out your time and save an hour or so for writing your stories, you will end up with many more pages than if you say, "Let's see how it goes, first, before I decide when I'll write."

The best place to write is a quiet one, a place you feel comfortable. (The places you may *end up* writing in are waiting rooms, uncleaned-up kitchens, parks, on planes, or even in the bathtub.) Take for yourself a corner, fix it up, and keep it for your writing place—a place where you don't have to keep putting everything away daily. A cardtable in the corner of your bedroom is fine. For empty–nesters, the best thing about your children's moving on to their own lives is that you get an empty room for another use, like writing.

Use the guest room if you have one. Or put your things in a portable carryall, briefcase, or artist's wooden box and set up on the deck when the weather is good.

A minimum number of pages per day? Certainly, if you are writing to sell. If you have another goal in mind, like putting together a booklet of stories for a reunion or for Christmas, figure out how many pages you'd need to do each day (include time for copying, drawing, assembling, etc., plus a few extra "unforseeable emergency" weeks).

Even if you are writing without a deadline, it's a good idea to commit yourself to several days a week, a couple of hours each day.

After you get caught up in the fever, you may find yourself writing more than your goal. If you are involved in a lot of projects and crafts, take a month and do nothing but writing. Then get on with other things until you can't stand it anymore, and write for another month.

Kim Stafford, one of the truly great inspirational writers, said: "The greatest sin against ourselves is to know what we want, and not to do it."

Do we want to pass on our **Heritage Memories?** Yes and more yes. Let's do it.

VII. FAVORITE RELATED BOOKS AND MATERIALS

Inspiration:

All But the Waltz, Mary Clearman Blew, Penguin Books, 1991

Creative Guide To Journal Writing, Dan Johnson, Gateway Pub., 1989

Families Writing, Peter R. Stillman, Writers Digest Books, 1989

Having Everything Right, Kim Stafford, Confluence Press, 1986

Love, Loss, and What I Wore, Ilene Beckerman, Algonquin of Chapel Hill, 1995

My Own Alphabet, Bobbie Louise Hawkins, Coffee House Press 1989

Opening Up: The Healing Power of Confiding in Others, James Pennebaker

Remember Who You Are, Esther Hautzig, Crown Publishers, 1990

Riding the White Horse Home, Teresa Jordan, Vintage/Random House, 1993

The Last Farmer, Howard Kohn, Harper & Row, 1988

The One-Room Schoolhouse, Jim Heynen, Knopf, 1993

To Our Children's Children, DG Fulford & Bob Greene, Doubleday, 1994

You Know What is Right, Jim Heynen, North Point Press, 1985

...And Instruction:

Family Tales, Family Wisdom, Dr. Robert Akenet, Morrow, 1991

How to Write your Own Life Story, Lois Daniel, Chicago Review Press, 1991

How to Write/Sell Your First Nonfiction Book, Collier & Leighton, St. Martin's, 1990

How to Write the Stories of Your Life, Frank Thomas, Writers Digest Books, 1984

How to Write/Sell Your Personal Experiences, Lois Duncan, Writers Digest Books, 1979

If You Want To Write, Brenda Ueland, Graywolf Press, 1987

The Writer in All of Us, Jane Gould, E.P. Dutton, 1981

Turning Life into Fiction, Robin Hemley, Story Press, 1994

Turning Memories into Memoirs, Denis Ledoux, Soleil Press, 1993

Unpuzzling Your Past, 3rd ed., Emily A. Crooms, Betterway Books, 1995

Wild Mind, Natalie Goldberg, Bantam, 1990

Write the Story of Your Life, Ruth Kanin, Hawthorn Dutton, 1981

Writing Articles From the Heart, Marjorie Holmes, Writers Digest Books, 1993

Writing Down the Bones, Natalie Goldberg, Shambala, 1986

Writing Across Cultures, Edna Kovacs, Blue Heron Press, 1994

Writing Personal Essays, Sheila Bender, Writers Digest Books, 1995

Writing After Fifty, Leonard Knott, Writers Digest Books, 1985

Writing Family Histories and Memoirs, Kirk Polking, Betterway Books, 1995

Writing as a Road to Self–Discovery, Barry Lane, Writers Digest Books, 1993

You Must Revise Your Life, William Stafford, The University of Michigan Press, 1986

References for Writing to Sell:

Almanacs, several kinds

AP Stylebook and Libel Manual (current edition)

Chicago Manual of Style, 14th edition, The University of Chicago Press, 1993

Chronicles, (20th cen., individ. year), by Chronicle Books

Dictionary, current and complete

How to Look It Up Online, A. Glossbrenner, St. Martin's Press

Pocket Speller, current, at least 25,000 words

Quotations/Anecdotes books

The Professional Writer's Guide, Bower & Young, National Writers Club, 1990

The Writer's Guide/From Prohibition through WWII, M. McCutcheon, WritersDigest Books, 1995

The Writing Business, editors of *Coda,* Poets & Writers/ Pushcart Press, 1985

The Writer's Guide to Everyday Life in the 1800s, McCutcheon, Writers Digest Books, 1993

The Encyclopedia of American Facts and Dates, 9th ed., Carruth,

The Writer's Guide to Manuscript Formats, Buchman & Groves, WritersDigest Books, 1987

The NY Public Library Book of Popular Americana, Tad Tuleja, Webster, 1994

The New York Public Library Desk Reference, Stonesong/ Webster's, 1989

The Timetables of History, Bernard Green, Simon & Schuster, 1982

The 30–Minute Writer, Connie Emerson, Writers Digest Books, 1993

Thesaurus

Timelines, Paul Dickson, Addison Wesley, 1991

Working With Words, Brooks and Pinson, St. Martin's Press 1989

Writer's Market (current year), Writers Digest Books

Ph-balanced Storage Materials:

Exposures catalog, 1-800-572-5750

(your Yellow Pages, your town's Historical Society and Genealogy groups)

Game:

Heritage Game (Sieben Hill)

ACKNOWLEDGEMENTS

It takes a whole village to raise a child, but generations influence the writing of a book on Heritage Writing.

A spiritual thankyou to those who have gone before us: Grandma R. and Grandma M., who told me stories on a regular basis; my parents. teachers, friends, and relatives who taught me the value of heritage stories and shared theirs with me.

Thanks to my agent, Anna Cottle, who walked me through book form on an earlier project; to Marlene Mahoney, whose interest in autobiography sparked mine; to Lee and Pastor Ed from the MacLaren School, who asked me to make more material on Heritage Writing available, and to F. W. who convinced me I could do it.

Of writers: Peter Sears years ago urged me to go public with my work; Jim Heynen, that master of the small tale, gave me more than I can describe on one page; Craig Lesley, with gentleness and skill honed the short story; Kim Stafford and Teresa Jordan inspired me greatly as they listened and shared their skills; Edna Kovacs opened the door to a side of writing I hadn't thought possible for just anyone to explore; and Scott Serpas let me count on him for suggestions and encouragement. Thanks to all of them.

Thank you to Dick and Mary Lutz, whose extraordinary patience and organization made the publishing process work.

The writer/publisher to whom I owe the most is Teresa Kao, who has unstintingly given of her time and talent to solve problems, and whose insight and encouragement are unmatched. Her friendship is greatly valued.

The grand prize of thankyous goes to my life-partner, Don, who has fulfilled many more roles than business manager, and whose love has been my mainstay through the writing of this book.

ORDER FORM

Name _____

Address _____

City/State/Zip _____

Phone _____

Enclosed is my check/money order for **$17.95** (**$14.95** for *HERITAGE WRITING* and $3 for shipping/handling).

SIEBEN HILL
P. O. Box 243
Clackamas, OR 97015-0243